so you wanna move to la

so you wanna move to la

Stories and Tips from a Professional Dancer

yoe apolinario

For anyone who feels personally attacked by "adulting."

contents

1
hello

My head swayed back and forth. Pins and needles ran through my fingers as images and colors blurred. I knew I was in for a wild night after three lines of cocaine. There I was, at a celebrity's house, high as a kite. Around 2 a.m., the Crips arrived to initiate me into their gang, but the ceremony was interrupted when a group of Bloods showed up and sprayed the whole mansion with gunfire. A bullet seared my leg in the chaos, and I woke up in the hospital a few days later. Though the doctors couldn't save my leg, I was still able to complete my initiation ceremony later on.

Okay, so that never happened. And by the grace of God, it never will. I've never used cocaine or been a Crip, but according to some of my family members and friends, that would be my fate upon moving to Los Angeles. To them, drug addiction and gang activity were inevitable. Though they never said this outright, they interwove their worries with all the advice and "facts" about Los Angeles they felt compelled to give me:

"Be careful with that cocaine stuff; it's really big out there!"

"Watch out for the gangs! Don't wear red or blue!"

One of my dance teachers said, "Just please be careful. I don't want you to become a drug addict!"

I would just nod and smile, pretending to take their advice, while on the inside I released ear-piercing screams. I wondered how they knew so much about a city they'd never lived in.

I'd learned not to do drugs in my adolescence. I'd managed to dodge gang life too. But I craved the advice that would actually prepare me to live in LA. I wish someone had warned me about the inflated cost of living. No one told me gas would be about two dollars higher than that of Tampa, Florida, my hometown. No one predicted that rent for a one-bedroom apartment in Van Nuys would be the same as my sister's mortgage for her brand-new three-bedroom house in Tampa.

I met people in LA who openly used cocaine and other drugs. Some nights, gunshots were a part of my neighborhood's soundtrack. But those experiences didn't trouble me as much as the time I sent $1,400 to a fake apartment landlord, or the terrible car insurance I purchased that didn't cover a cent when I got into a fender bender.

My loved ones had good intentions, and their concerns were valid. Drug abuse and gang activity are real issues in LA County. Within five minutes of driving into downtown LA, you'll likely spot a homeless person who's under the influence, mentally ill, or both, talking to themselves or yelling at an invisible aggressor.

In the six years I've lived here, I haven't experienced a Bloods-versus-Crips brawl, but I'm sure it's possible.

People wanted to educate me on the risks of drugs but fell silent when it came to the skills I'd need to survive in a new city. Few offered me wisdom about building credit, managing money, or purchasing a car. I was young when I moved here and hadn't hit those milestones yet. So now, in this book, I want to tell you everything I never knew before moving to LA so that you don't have to figure it out on your own.

My name is Yoe Apolinario, and I'm a professional dancer based out of Los Angeles, California. Since moving here from Tampa in 2015, I've had the opportunity to work with artists like Chris Brown, H.E.R., Taylor Swift, the Backstreet Boys, and more. I've traveled all over the world and danced behind artists in music videos and on tours.

I'm considered one of the lucky ones. After I moved out here with about eight thousand dollars in savings, work came my way almost immediately. About four months later, I booked my first tour where I built my savings even more. And after one of the biggest tours of my career, I purchased a townhome in an over-priced LA housing market. I never had to get a regular job; by "regular," I mean a nine-to-five, inflexible office or service job. By the grace of God, all my side hustles have been compatible with the ever-changing schedule of a professional dancer. That's rare out here in these streets.

On paper, my life in LA looks nothing short of a dream. And in many ways, it has been. It probably looks easy and free of hardship, as if everything was given to me. But boy, was that not the case. I like to describe LA as an eternal roller coaster. Emotions, finances, health—they all go on one big, wild ride. It can be hard as hell. I wish somebody had warned me about a fraction of the things I would experience here. While apartment hunting, breaking into the industry, or even trying to shop on a budget, I wish I'd had some sort of guidance. In addition to hard-core adulting, I also had to learn how to navigate the world of celebrities and musical artists.

This book includes real-life experiences from my career. Some actual names will be used, but most will be fake. Try to refrain from becoming Sherlock Holmes and attempting to piece the true names together. Instead, focus on the lessons you can take from each story.

I wrote this book for anyone who wants to make the move to La-La Land. For anyone who wants to pursue a career in professional dance or the entertainment industry. For anyone who wants to move to a big city and be the small, new fish in a huge pond.

Welcome.

Before moving forward, please note:

Fulana (feminine) or Fulano (masculine), in Puerto Rican culture, is another way of saying "what's-her-name" or "what's-his-name." It's synonymous with "that person" or "young man/young lady." Similar to the filler name "Jane Doe."

2
fired

No matter what, you're going to experience some
type of L in this career. A loss in the form of a
no, a talent release, or a plain ol' "You're fired."
You can't avoid it. All that matters is how you
get through it and move forward.

One by one, I scanned the dancers' Instagram stories: A picture of a plane wing from the window seat. A funny clip of a female dancer fast asleep at the gate with a pink neck pillow cradling her head. A male dancer having a drink at the bar before boarding. He'd captioned the picture, "The only way to do an international flight," along with a martini-glass emoji. All the dancers I'd been rehearsing with for the past few weeks were on their way to a concert, where they'd be dancing alongside a major artist.

The only thing was, I never received a plane ticket. The artist's management hadn't sent me anything remotely close to a ticket or a flight confirmation. I wouldn't be boarding the flight all the other dancers were boarding because I was just at home, watching from my phone and connecting the dots.

That's how I found out I was fired.

I refreshed my coworkers' profiles every two minutes, yearning for an explanation. Maybe half of the dancers were leaving today and the rest would depart tomorrow; surely I'd be part of the second group. Yet every update and post proved me wrong. All the dancers were at the airport—all of them except for me.

I'd spent the past two weeks with them, tirelessly rehearsing for an international show. Those eight-to-twelve-hour rehearsals, six days a week, planted seeds that had bloomed into bonds. I got to know everyone on an individual level. I learned about Becca's plan to get married and Tiana's worries about moving in with her boyfriend. We all had different dance backgrounds, so we'd spend the beginning of each rehearsal warming up and learning from one another. I found my wine buddy and my smoking buddy.

It wasn't all roses, though. Every artist has their quirks, but working with Etta was especially difficult. She demanded a lot whether she was present or not. Our call time was five to six hours before hers. We used that time to perfect the dance routines before her arrival, but Etta never actually made it to rehearsal on time. She'd float in two or three hours late with a random story, antsy child, or some other larger-than-life antic at hand.

Sometimes she'd lie down in the middle of the dance floor and talk about the most random topics, interrupting the day's flow. Or she'd drift into the band's space for a few hours, leading an impromptu session or trying to learn how to play a new instrument.

Other days, she'd show up with her kids, two cute little brown-skinned bundles of joy between the ages of six and nine who had the energy of a dozen Tasmanian devils. They sang and stole our phones while rampaging through the entire rehearsal room. Even the nanny had trouble keeping up. I loved them, but they were always a complete waste of time. That was no worry for Etta, though. Whenever the day's distraction ended, we'd begin rehearsal and finish whenever she pleased.

It had been brutal, but that part was over. We'd finished LA rehearsals and now it was time to board a fourteen-hour flight overseas, rehearse at the venue for a week, and perform. Or so I thought. Once I'd spent two hours mindlessly refreshing their profiles, I decided to accept the reality that I was let go from the job. I had to calm my mind, so I did what I always do when my life feels crazy: I took my dog to the park.

Drool rained from Lupe's mouth onto the grass. Despite having fetched the ball a hundred times, she wasn't tired of playing. I'd arrived at the park with my chest and shoulders feeling tight and rigid, but they were loosening as time went on. Lupe helped clear my mind of it all. Every time I chucked the ball across the empty park, she sprinted with the same vigor, her ears flopping with every gallop and her tongue dangling in the wind. The sheer joy pouring from her body ceased my anxiety. Maybe Sheepadoodles really are therapy animals.

Engulfed in her world, I captured a short video of Lupe running back with the ball in her mouth. At the end of the video she dropped the ball at my feet, looked up, and tilted her head to the side. It was just the cutest moment! With a smile from ear to ear, I posted the video to my Instagram story.

Ping! Within two minutes, a notification displayed on my phone screen. It was a message from Josh, a dancer on the Etta job.

JOSH

Aren't flying out today?

ME

No, are you flying out today? I never received a flight confirmation.

JOSH

What??? Oh noooo.

I locked the screen and stored my phone in my purse. I didn't need to read anymore. He knew exactly what no flight confirmation meant.

Worn out by the mental roller coaster I'd endured for the past few hours, I spent the rest of the day distracting my mind.

Months later, I was at my friend Brianna's house catching up. She belongs to the generation of dancers before me; she'd danced with Etta years before it was even a thought in my mind. The conversation began with a few unimportant events in my life and somehow evolved into a play-by-play of the day I was fired.

As soon as I mentioned Josh's name, Brianna interrupted me. "Josh? The guy from Chicago with the high-top fade? Girl, you know Etta is dating him on the low. That's probably why she fired you. That natural beauty of yours must've had her sick to her stomach."

A distant ringing sound swam through my ears. My surroundings slowed for a couple of seconds. *Dating him on the low?! What in the world?!* I flashed back to my experiences with Josh during those weeks of rehearsal. How could Etta have suspected something between Josh and me? If she'd spent two seconds asking me or investigating on social media, she would've quickly learned that I was a lesbian. I'd never had much contact with...

Oh, no, I thought. *The night of the party. That had to be the night that changed everything.*

After we'd completed the LA rehearsals, Etta threw a small celebration in the private room of a club. Seeing as how she never showed us too much affection, I thought the party was a little odd. Still, I decided not to dwell on it.

A few thousand indecisive outfit changes later, I strolled into the club and through the gold-rimmed double doors that led to a private VIP room.

Measuring somewhere between five hundred and seven

hundred square feet, the private room wasn't too large, but there was a free buffet, and that's what mattered most. Etta was sitting in a booth in deep conversation with Corey, the choreographer. The room was the size of a large studio apartment, but those two were in their own world. I decided I would say hello later.

All the dancers were on the dance floor, drinks in hand and hips winding to the beat. My eyes immediately locked with Tiana's.

"Yoeeeeee! I was starting to think you weren't coming!" She stumbled over to me with a margarita in one hand and the other stretched out.

"Girl, me too! I was really struggling. I had no idea what to wear!" I said as we embraced each other.

Tiana scanned the lace bodysuit hugging my curves, the navy-blue two-piece suit on top of it, and the all-black Jordans— my version of dressy yet comfy.

She shook her head. "Didn't know what to wear?! Well, damn, the wait was worth it 'cause that outfit is bomb!"

"Aw, thanks boo! I'm just trying to keep up with you!"

"No problem! Go get you a drink. It's an open bar."

"Open bar? Say less!"

I excused myself and paraded toward the bar. At first, I hadn't planned to drink; our call time was 8 a.m. the next morning, and I needed an alcohol-free body to survive. But I also live by the motto "Free is for me," and free alcohol is most definitely for me.

One drink will be my cap, I declared. *I have a joint in my purse. I'll have one mojito, step outside to smoke, ravage the buffet, and dance with the rest of the cast—the perfect plan.*

The bar was no more than five feet away from where I had my moment with Tiana, but I wouldn't get there until twenty minutes later. One by one, the rest of the dancers greeted me. We hugged, complimented each other, and had spurts of small talk. All the topics of conversation were different, but one thing was for sure: Everyone was drunk. Not tipsy, but stumbling, mic-less karaoke-singing, permanent-smile *drunk*. They did not come to play with this open bar! If I didn't transform into a creature from hangovers and a lack of sleep, I would've been right on their level. For now, my pint-sized, over-iced mojito and a sativa joint would supply the buzz.

After downing the cocktail in three sips, I slipped out the side exit. With the joint propped behind my ear, I rummaged through my purse in search of a lighter.

"Ayeeee, I'm about to smoke too," a voice called out.

I lifted my eyes from my purse to spot Josh a few yards away, walking toward me. He'd also arrived fashionably late.

"So what we doing?!" I yelled.

Josh is a very talented dancer. Artistry and creativity seem to ooze from his pores when he moves. His unique, textured style sets him apart from most of the males in the industry.

It wasn't his style that drew me to him, though. The first time our paths crossed was at a dance event in LA a couple of years back. Having only lived in the City of Angels for two years by that point, I was still just a tadpole in a humongous pond.

There was a plethora of people I hadn't met and a hundred events I had yet to attend.

My wife and I were in our early stages, and she'd constructed a mini date night out of the whole ordeal. We'd have dinner near the event a couple of hours before it began, sip on some cocktails at a bar, then dance the night away with other members of the community.

After filling our tummies and drinking a couple of cocktails, we entered the event. Bodies were rhythmically moving in all directions, and a deep-house bass reverberated through our bones. In an instant the music took over. SHE and I exchanged movement back and forth as if it was our own language. Her movement was like the rapid sections of a river: riveting and exciting, but outright dangerous. Words left her limbs and somehow I understood what they meant, enough to reply with my own language of movement. I was mesmerized, and others were too. I'm not sure when it happened, but a crowd of observers surrounded our conversation, forming a large circle with us in the center. They had front-row seats to our little world.

One by one, other dancers stepped into our world and joined our exchange. Instead of the conversation bouncing between SHE and me, it moved from SHE, to a female dancer, to a male dancer, to me, to another female, and back to SHE again. For much of the session, each dancer remained internal, the conversation flowing between them and the music. They'd fixate their eyes on something in the room or on the floor, exploring, getting lost in themselves. I was in awe at what the session had become.

At the end of someone's round, a tall brown-skinned man emerged from the crowd. He entered the center of the circle and immediately felt the music. He began mimicking the background beats with his hand, the energy traveling throughout his body. Although he was dancing, it felt like he was telling a story. And while he told this story, his eyes were glued to one person: SHE. He moved his long limbs in every which direction—toward the floor, around different points of the circle, back to the center—all while never breaking his gaze from SHE. Was this a call-out battle?

As imaginary claws expanded from my knuckles, the man danced to the opposite side of the circle, ended his round, and took a knee. He fanned his arms up and down toward SHE as if he was saying, "All hail the Queen." My imaginary claws contracted in a flash. What I thought was a call-out actually turned out to be a display of affection—not in the sense of love or intimacy, but as a declaration of respect. He was showing endless humility because talent-wise, he and SHE were from the same planet. This exchange didn't fall heavily toward one side. No one beat the other; no one was more talented. It was an even scale.

In the middle of his praise, she pulled him off the floor and into a hug.

"Oh, get off the floor! It's been so long since I've seen you!" she said.

Oh, they know each other? I thought.

After their embrace unraveled, SHE stepped back and went off, hitting and moving to the beat. The young man got back down on his knee with a sparkle in his eye. I'll never forget the way he watched her, with respect and admiration practically oozing from him.

My protective nature had been so quick to classify this young man as one of her haters. I laughed at the escalated scene I'd developed in my mind. Later that night, SHE told me the mystery man's identity. His name was Josh, and they'd met at an out-of-town dance battle years ago.

From that night on, Josh was one of my favorite male dancers. Not because of his talent, though he was abnormally gifted, but because his heart seemed pure. He was a true lover of the art. While he watched SHE dance, I saw not the slightest hint of ego or comparison. A lot of people are talented in the industry; that's not hard to come by. But it's rare to find people who are both confident and humble, who don't question their own light while in the presence of others. Josh observed SHE in total awe and while completely assured of his gift. After that moment, we spent most of the night exchanging to every track the DJ played.

Months later, when I nervously entered a rehearsal space with Etta, an artist who was notorious for her peculiar ways, I stuck by the first familiar face in the room: Josh. After a few weeks of rehearsal, I'd established connections with the other dancers on the job, but I felt an unspoken comfort with Josh. This was partly because I'd known him longer, but also because I get excited about guy friends, especially the ones I don't have to worry about.

You know the worries tickling the back of your subconscious: Does he have a crush on me? Is he pretending to be friends as he patiently waits for my lesbianism to "disappear"? As outlandish as it may seem, I've experienced it. Josh's heart-filled respect for Sheopatra's craft told me he would respect her relationship as well. I felt safe with him and never worried that he'd try anything out of the blue. So when he joined me for a smoking session on the night of that party, I welcomed him with open arms.

When we returned from outside, our vision tunneled toward the buffet. Without a word, we floated past all the dancers on the dance floor and straight to the food. Section by section, we filled our plates with all the night's selections and sat at the first open table. I'm not sure how we managed, but five plates sat between us. And once again without a word, we dug in our forks and ate everything in sight. With red eyes and our bodies succumbing to the effects of marijuana, we giggled at nothing and ate like the food was fine dining. His fork traveled to my plate and my fork traveled to his, testing all the foods we hadn't initially chosen.

After demolishing all the food in sight, we decided to take pictures. Both styled in suits, we posted up beside the table with ultimate boss energy as one of our fellow dancers played photographer. Laughter erupted as soon as we saw that picture. Josh's eyes are small by nature, but they looked completely closed, clearly giving away our previous smoke break. It was funny, no doubt, but the cannabis amped up the humor of it all, igniting our gut-wrenching laughter. In between laughs, I came up for air.

"Here, take my glasses. They'll hide how high you look," I said.

He put them on and felt the vibes instantly—the vibes one gets when they *know* they look stylish—causing me to chuckle even more. Somehow, I pulled myself together enough to take another picture.

While we posed, a feeling came over me and I knew that somebody was looking at me. After the flash of our last photo, I scanned the small room and met Etta's harsh, wintry gaze. Her stare—almost identical to that of a childhood staring contest, minus the fun—cut through my eyes like daggers. Why was she looking at me like that? As soon as our eyes met, I turned away and pretended not to notice. Yet nothing stopped the ice I felt from her glare.

Seconds later, a few dancers sauntered off the dance floor toward our table.

"Come on!" Tiana slurred. "Let's dance!"

And then I was on the dance floor, poppin', lockin', and droppin' it like it was hot. Despite being professionals, we didn't take anything too seriously and let a playful air surround our moves. We performed the sprinkler, the running man, and bad booty-shaking. We walked imaginary runways and rotated like models on a catwalk.

Then the DJ played a track with an infectious bass. Afro house filled my ears, my body. Before I knew it, my dancing was no longer playful. I distanced myself from the rest of the dancers, allowing myself to explore the music. Beat by beat, my body reacted to the rhythm.

A few dancers surrounded me, and Josh took a front-row position. After about forty-five seconds, I brought my round to a close and transferred the energy to him. He accepted the energy and let the music enter his body.

Twenty minutes later, beads of sweat had formed on our foreheads as the pattern continued. I danced, then he danced. Footwork guided my steps. Footwork guided his. I geared my movement toward the floor. So did he. After my last round, my lungs gasping for air, I headed to the open bar and unscrewed the first water bottle in sight.

While I gulped down water in between breaths, my mind wandered. I was so grateful to be on a job with a freestyler as talented as Josh. Most of my jobs involve dancers whose expertise lies solely in choreography. Some artists are paid to paint whatever the buyer wants, like something in nature or a skateboard mural for a shop. Then there are artists who move straight from the dome. They paint whatever comes to mind, and no matter what, it'll be so profound that someone will pay for it.

One isn't easier than the other. As a dancer who grew up in the rigid studio world learning and being told how to dance, the transition to the hip-hop freestyle world was drastic. I didn't know how to move without specific instructions; I couldn't move freely. But after a couple of years of intense training, it became one of my favorite pastimes, so I'm overjoyed when I'm on a job with another freestyler. During long breaks and warm-ups, I have the opportunity to take a mental break from the rigorous world of memorization and eight counts, and I can do so with another dancer. Dancing with him was just so much fun, so freeing, much needed, and—

What is Etta looking at?

Etta's big brown eyes were once again glaring at me from across the room. She was whispering into Corey's ear as his eyes bounced from Etta to me.

I'd had enough. The tension weighed a ton in that tiny room. Unsure of what to do next, I threw away the water bottle and joined the other dancers on the dance floor, this time with a simple two-step.

Maybe I was dancing too hard... Maybe I'd drawn too much attention to myself...

My limbs softly rocked from side to side. But on the inside, my mind jump-roped through all the possible reasons Etta had stared at me for that long when she'd never looked at me before.

Perhaps it was a coping mechanism, or she was just uncomfortable with new faces, but Etta hadn't looked at me for the entire rehearsal process. She never made eye contact with me or the other new dancers on the job. She knew our names, of course, but never addressed us directly. Corey acted as the buffer.

While observing our pieces, she whispered critiques into a microphone:

"Corey, can you move Yoe to the right a little bit?"

"Corey, Fulana looks out of place. Can you fix the formation?"

When dealing with her veteran dancers, though, she spoke

with unwavering eye contact. She was comfortable with them, though some might argue she was *too* comfortable.

"Fulano, I never want to see your legs again. No more basketball shorts."

"Fulana, your hair is all over the place. Wear it different tomorrow."

To maintain my mental stability, I had to squeeze the humor out of these situations. So after the first few remarks, I categorized her as an auntie. You know the outspoken auntie (or any other family member) who spits out their immediate opinion without the slightest regard for others. The auntie who comments on your weight or hair at family functions. The auntie who says, "Oh, you and that boy broke up? Oh, good, 'cause he wasn't all that handsome anyhow."

Unsolicited opinions were the peanut butter to Etta's jelly. One couldn't exist without the other. I learned that very quickly.

During costume fittings, she'd inspect us in a military-style horizontal line. One by one, she and the head of the wardrobe department evaluated each dancer, with the head of wardrobe meticulously noting all of Etta's requests.

"Can we get another skirt for her? This one doesn't show off her long legs."

"Let's take in his jacket a little."

She is, by far, one of the most demanding artists I've ever worked for, but I applaud how involved she was in the entire process. Many artists reside in their own worlds without a care for how their team looks. It's common for an artist to be decked out in designer gear from head to toe, surrounded by dancers styled in Forever 21's best.

Etta spared no expense on her dancers. We wore unique, handcrafted costumes. Though they made me feel like I was standing on rigid wooden boards for hours, Gucci shoes covered our feet. Etta is crazy, but it works sometimes. She wanted us to look as put together as her.

When they'd made their way down the line to me, Etta gave the stylist her feedback. "Let's lose the top. Keep the skirt. Find a more colorful top instead."

She scanned my body up and down, each time diverting her gaze away from my eyes. That's how Etta had always dealt with me, taking in the space around me but never making eye contact. So when she served me a chilling glare from across that tiny club, my mind froze over.

I did my best not to dwell on it. I step-touched with the other dancers, allowing the moves to silence my thoughts. Tiana pulled me into an embrace as we step-touched together. When we separated, a new body was on the dance floor: Corey. His body swayed from side to side inches away from Tiana and me. We smiled and joined his rhythm.

"Ah, I just love this song!" he shouted over the music.

"Me, too! It's a hit!" I replied.

Tiana had already begun her hug step-touch combo with another dancer. Corey floated closer to me, never missing a beat, continuing his bop.

He leaned into me and asked, "You like women, right?"

"Yeah…"

I wasn't sure what to make of this question. Corey knew about Sheopatra; he'd commented on a couple of our relationship pictures, for heaven's sake! And I knew for a fact that Corey didn't bat for the same team as me. I'd worked with a lot of his exes, all gorgeous black men.

"Just women? You don't like guys at all?"

"Uh... I mean... I've had a boyfriend before, but most of my exes are women."

"Oh, okay."

And just like that, the conversation ended as strangely as it had begun, with Corey swaying away to the beat. He moved on to a new group of dancers, feeling the bass with them. I, however, did *not* move on. An instinctual buzz forced my body to continue dancing to the beat, perhaps to shield my discomfort from the other dancers who were probably too enveloped in their worlds to notice. My feet performed chill party grooves while my brain performed somersaults.

Why would he ask me questions like that?

"Damn, that's crazy," Brianna said after I'd recalled the events between Josh and me. Her hands twisted and turned around my last braid. "So no one told her you were gay?"

"I don't know what they told her. Corey could have told her, but maybe she didn't care. Or maybe Corey didn't believe me. It's just... How do you date someone you *know* is jealous and still hang with me like that?! Like, if you know your girl—or girlfriend boss—is crazy, don't drag me into that. Stay away from me!" My skin grew hot.

"Yeah, he was wrong. And Etta's wrong for messing with that boy, but she is crazy. Everybody knows that."

I sighed. Tension released from my shoulders, though I hadn't noticed it there to begin with.

"You're right. Etta *is* crazy, and I'm not sure how many more jobs I could've done with her. Maybe being fired was meant to be."

3
the draft

During the first days of freshman year, my high school hosted a group of guests in the cafeteria. They occupied their own table, spoke to students as they passed by, and delivered one-liners that were sure to get the student body's attention:

"Wanna get your college paid for?"

"It doesn't matter if your grades are low!"

"Do you want to travel?"

"The Army might be the place for you."

Though their sales pitch was identical to that of someone selling a timeshare, they caught my attention. After getting food from the lunch line and scanning the room for my friends, my eyes paused at their table. I stared at their uniforms and pamphlets like I hadn't seen them the day before. After about a week, the guests moved on, probably to another school in the district, but their promises floated in the back of my mind.

That first year of high school felt like an ocean. My options felt as endless as the depths of the sea. The waves moved me toward one career option, then another, then another. Though some options were sure to drown me in stress and debt if I chose them.

Teachers, guidance counselors, and administrators were like storms disrupting our boats, constantly reminding us to "Think about what you wanna do after high school!" and "Start planning for it now!" Words of encouragement that were meant to keep us focused bred nothing but angst and anxiety within me.

I couldn't imagine going to school for more than six years, so getting a doctorate was out of the question. I thought about becoming a medical assistant like my mom or a registered nurse like many of the Latinas around me. But the thought of paying for a college education tormented me. There was no way my parents could fund my education, so I would have to take out a loan. Horror stories of college students graduating with two hundred thousand dollars in debt rang in my ears like a scary nursery rhyme.

It only took a month for me to heavily consider enlisting in the military after graduation. Because I danced, I was in pretty good shape, so I figured basic training wouldn't be too bad. Getting up early might be difficult, but if I could make it to the bus stop by 6 a.m. every morning, then the military might be bearable. In addition to paid college tuition, a friend of mine told me there were other benefits, such as cheaper housing and free health insurance. That was all my fifteen-year-old, first-generation-immigrant ears needed to hear. Army, Navy, Air Force, Marines—I couldn't tell the difference between them, but I didn't care. I wanted those benefits. I craved that stability.

On Career Day, the guests returned with additional tables. Instead of passing them by, this time I took control. I spoke to sergeants, grabbed handfuls of pamphlets, and even joined a pull-up contest for a free pizza. I tried to join ROTC, but I didn't have room in my schedule. (At my school, dance majors didn't have room for other electives since ballet, modern, and dance kinesiology took up all our slots. We had to dedicate the rest of our schedules to academic courses.) I was disappointed, but one of the sergeants reassured me that I didn't have to join ROTC to enlist in the military after school. He encouraged me to continue as a dance major and enjoy high school in the meantime.

In hindsight, I'm thankful for that sergeant. While the others encouraged me to change my major the following semester, he was the only one who advised me otherwise. I like to think God worked through that man, nudging me in the right direction before I veered too far off.

4

where is she?

N one of my teachers had assigned homework, so this Friday felt extra sweet. As soon as I stepped foot in my home, I threw my backpack into my room, shut the door, and looked forward to the weekend, even though I wouldn't have too much freedom. On Saturdays, dance practice ran from 9 a.m. to 2 p.m., followed by a two-hour rehearsal on Sunday, but I couldn't care less. I desperately needed a break from school.

I rummaged through the fridge and found the ingredients to make an award-winning after-school snack. With an orange soda in one hand and a sandwich in the other, I plopped onto the living room recliner and let the soothing sounds of *106 & Park* play on the TV. A spa treatment to my sixteen-year-old mind. In what felt like the blink of an eye, nighttime fell. Soon my grandma came into the house with containers full of leftover dinner from her house. The smells drew the rest of my siblings out of their rooms.

"Hey, have you seen your mom?" she asked.

I glanced at the clock: 8:15 p.m.

"No, I thought she was at the store or something," I said. My siblings echoed my answer.

Mami had a habit of disappearing after clocking out of work at five. We'd worry about her, but then she'd waltz in seconds later carrying countless bags from Ross or Walmart—evidence of her whereabouts. In my adulthood, I learned that these quiet retail splurges were coping mechanisms for her depression, but back then we figured she just liked to shop.

"Hmm... Okay."

"Did you call her?" I asked.

"Yeah, but you know your mom. She never answers the phone." A fact that remains true to this day.

By the time 10 p.m. rolled around, my grandmother was sitting at the kitchen table in full investigation mode. By calling Mami's coworkers, she learned that Mami never made it to work that morning. She called local hospitals asking if someone by the name of Awilda Renovales had checked in. So far, no hospital had any record of a patient with that name.

Where is she? I wondered. Waves of panic prickled my skin as my mind conjured up worst-case scenarios. *What's the next step? Do we call the police? Do we go looking for her? Do we—?*

"She's there?" my grandma said into the phone. "Okay. Okay. We'll be right there."

Turns out, my mother had checked herself into the hospital

at around 4 a.m. I'd grown so accustomed to having no time to spare before school, always jogging to the bus stop in a state of panic as it arrived, that I hadn't noticed the empty driveway that morning.

———

Mami lay in the hospital bed, nodding yes or no while jumbled grunts and sentence fragments left her mouth. No matter how hard she tried, she couldn't move her left arm. The left side of her face drooped slightly, and a swollen black-and-blue knot sat on top of her cheekbone. Her left leg wasn't moving either; when it was time for her to use the restroom, she needed all the surrounding adults to help her. Most of her left side wasn't moving, but the right side functioned normally. Almost like her body was divided right down the middle.

Mami had been sick before. She'd visited hospitals more often after RJ was born in 2003; she'd checked herself into the emergency room then too. But this time was different. It was 2011, and I'd never, ever in my life seen her this bad. To this day, the memory of Mami in that hospital bed can still make my eyes water.

I excused myself to the waiting room, desperate to hear the reason for all of this. The first theory was that she'd had a stroke. Mami had already been diagnosed with a heart condition, so it made the most sense to doctors. But various tests and brain scans revealed the real cause: her multiple sclerosis had relapsed, an illness my siblings and I didn't even know she had, because she'd hidden her 2003 diagnosis from us.

Multiple sclerosis, or MS, is an autoimmune disorder that affects the nervous system throughout the body. It causes an array of symptoms anywhere one has nerves, which is *everywhere*. MS can come and go in waves, similar to asthma or allergies. Though the symptoms might not show, it's always there, dormant until triggered. Some of the worst things for people with MS are heat, alcohol, and stress. Mami is a Puerto Rican dance and baseball mom living in Florida, who had four mouths to feed at the time. Heat, alcohol, and stress were part of her everyday life!

However, that year her stress levels reached an all-time high. Just a couple of months before, immigration officers had arrested my stepfather, Roberto, where he worked.

I'll never forget that day. It was one of the chosen Saturdays Roberto had clocked into a short shift at work. For some reason, dance practice was canceled that day, so I settled into my favorite spot on the living room recliner and watched TV.

The home phone served no purpose in my household: it was an unwanted, debt collector–ridden, emergencies-only trap. Only four or five calls came through a day, but we ignored them all with vigor. We only had that phone because it was included in an affordable phone, internet, and cable bundle. So each time it rang, we continued with our day.

Fifteen minutes into my show, the phone rang. I cranked up the volume on the TV to drown out the tone coming from the kitchen. About ten minutes later, the phone rang again. Two hours later, I had counted nine calls in total.

Debt collectors must be extra diligent today, I thought. *They've never called this many times before. Some people need to get a life!*

I threw the remote down and walked past the kitchen where my mom was looking in the fridge for something to cook.

"Good morning, Mami."

"Buenos días, mi amor."

As I walked toward the restroom, that dreadful phone rang again.

"Coño, este jodio teléfono has been going off all morning!" Mami roared in perfect Spanglish.

I suppressed the snicker trying to escape my mouth. Right before I closed the bathroom door, I heard my mother assume her professional voice.

"Hello, this is Windy. Who's speaking?"

Though I hadn't planned to, I spent a lot of time in the restroom. I plucked my eyebrows, applied product to my curls, and picked at a few pimples collecting at the corner of my chin. By the time I left, Mami wasn't on the phone anymore. I assumed she'd sent those debt collectors pa la pinga and started cooking lunch. But when I returned to the kitchen, Mami's upper body was slumped over the counter, her head resting in her folded arms while muffled sobs escaped her. For the first time in my sixteen years on earth, I witnessed my mother, a woman who never cried, bawling her eyes out.

"Mami! What happened?!"

She lifted her body. Her red, puffy eyes stared directly into me. "They took him."

"Who?! Mami, they took who?!"

"Immigración. They detained Roberto at his job this morning."

For some reason, the only contact number Roberto's job had was the house phone. That's who had called so many times. They wanted to notify us as soon as possible that they were taking Roberto to a detention center ten hours away in Louisiana.

From then on, things changed. Mami spent a lot of time on the phone. With 60 percent of the household income gone, money became tighter than ever. And eventually her health suffered as well, reigniting her multiple sclerosis.

———

The morning she checked herself into the hospital, Mami stepped out of bed, but her left leg, which was unknowingly paralyzed, did not respond. It couldn't bear the weight of her body, causing her to fall. Her brain commanded her left arm to reach out and break the fall, but her left arm was also unresponsive, leaving her left cheekbone to take all the force. She stretched her right arm up, reaching for anything to grab a hold of. Once she was able to hoist herself up on the bed, she noticed that something else was terribly wrong: No matter how many times she blinked, nothing cleared her post-sleep grogginess. She couldn't see. Double vision invaded her left eye. Trying to remain as calm as possible, she put on a robe, grabbed her purse, hobbled to the car on her right leg, and drove herself to the hospital, struggling to distinguish between the double vision in her left eye and the normal sight in her right eye.

On our way to the hospital, my grandma finally got in contact with Mami's nurse, who recounted the events to her: the paralysis in her left side, the double vision, and the trouble speaking. But they still didn't know why her cheekbone was bruised. Those details wouldn't be revealed until months later once Mami had regained her speech.

Nothing but rage filled my body during that car ride. No matter how much I tried, I couldn't understand why someone with a husband and a family would disappear into the night without uttering a simple "call my family" upon arrival at the hospital. She could've written a note to the nurses with the same right hand that had helped her drive there. *Something!* Instead she chose to remain undiscoverable until the evening. Had she hoped to return home before anyone noticed? My grandmother lived two streets away and was more than capable of driving Mami to the ER. Why did she so recklessly choose to drive with only one good eye? I was furious. But the moment I set eyes on my mother, that fury evaporated, only to be replaced with horror.

The shock of seeing Mami in such a vegetative state didn't dissipate until six months later as she learned to walk and talk again. But then new pressures set in, like our household going from two incomes, to one income, and finally—for almost a year—to no income. As the weeks passed, we realized the odds of her returning to work weren't so good. Her road to rehabilitation was all uphill, and Roberto was still in a detention center. Quickly, Mami realized the income issues in our home might not be so temporary after all.

Because my high school had a magnet performing arts program, they bussed in children from all over the county, even though it was thirty minutes away from my house. The school district provided transportation to and from classes, but anything outside of that, such as extracurriculars, was the sole responsibility of our parents.

In the fall, I was on Sting, the marching band's dance team. Not only did I stay after school to rehearse during the week, but we attended band camp for two weeks in the middle of summer vacation. For all of those practices, Mami dropped me off and picked me up.

During the school day, I was a dance major, and dance majors studied ballet and modern. That was it. No other styles of dance were considered "serious disciplines." They might've spoiled us with a hip-hop guest teacher from time to time. But in their eyes, hip-hop wasn't a fine art; it was just something to treat us with, like a pizza party. From 3 p.m., when the final bell rang, till 6 p.m., I entered the world of the marching band: a mixture of jazz, hip-hop, majorette, and drill.

During the fall, Mami had to pick me up from band practice. In March and April, the dance majors' spring concert rolled around, which was another after-school endeavor. And during the final months of school, from May to June, the senior dance majors put together their own choreography showcase where they cast students for their pieces—yet another reason Mami had to make that infamous drive. Because of all this, I rarely utilized the bus system. After my extracurriculars, I attend classes at a local dance school until 9 p.m. Mami was my transportation for all of it.

Once that school year ended, Mami had two requests: that I take a break from the dance studio next year and go to a high school closer to home. Dance classes and competitive teams were expensive enough for one child, but my mom was responsible for both my younger sibling Jaz's and my training. The studio owner had been lenient given the situation, but Mami didn't want her debt to grow any larger. And with her fluctuating health and perpetual doctor's appointments, the odds of Mami being able to pick me up from a school thirty minutes away were slim to none.

I sat still that summer. No dance workshops, no competitions, no traveling for shows or classes. I just stayed home, strategically picking my Top 8 on Myspace and talking with my cousin on the phone. When the school year started, I went to a school ten minutes away from my house, took the bus home at the end of the day, and resumed the same routine.

Dance conventions exposed me to the possibility of making dance a career. I wasn't just reading articles or watching documentaries; I was taking classes from the choreographers and backup dancers for the biggest celebrities at the time, right there in the flesh. They made that unobtainable dream a reality, or at least *somewhat* of a reality.

As a first-generation kid from a family of immigrants, I

wasn't taught to dream very often. It wasn't because my parents didn't believe in me; it was because they loved me. They loved me so much that they prayed for my life to be easier than theirs. Going to college, learning a trade, living life with a substantial income and free from any of the struggles they faced—this was the attitude adopted by my extended family, aunts, uncles, and grandparents. My mom lived by these words: "I don't care if my daughter ends up a stripper as long as she's the best stripper at the damn club!"

Her support gave me a boost, a little kick inside saying, "You can do it if you really want to!" But when the bills piled up and it became hard to put food on the table, I was forced to confront the reality: If I chose to move to LA to pursue dance, she couldn't pay my rent for the first year, buy my car, or furnish my apartment like some of my friends' parents could. I would be on my own. That's what made something like joining the Army sound like the better option. It gave birth to the little voice in my head that said, "Do dance as a hobby. But when you graduate, find a real job and make some money."

That had been the plan since freshman year. But in my junior year, after about four months without dance, I felt empty. Depressed. Without purpose. Only four months had passed when I realized I couldn't imagine a life without dance in some form.

I decided to meet with my studio owner and ask for a scholarship in exchange for teaching children's classes. She doubled my offer, granting me the scholarship and paying me to teach. God bless her and the dozens of people who poured into me around this time. Though I only earned about sixty dollars a week, I was able to provide family dinner from time to time.

Eventually the studio owner covered both my class tuition and competition dues. I'll never forget the feeling of being back in class those first couple of weeks. I was going wild! Dancing full-out without being told, challenging myself to do more than I had before. The feeling was different this time around. I *wanted* to be there. I'd made the choice, as opposed to doing so because Mami could pay for it. I tried harder and harder every day because in the back of my mind, I knew there was no way I could give it up. I was moving to LA.

5
the grind

During the second half of my junior year, I decided that moving to LA meant compromises had to be made.

I had to fulfill the immigrant dream of receiving a college education and save money to cover the move to California. With the help of my guidance counselor, I added dual-enrollment courses to my schedule, which allowed me to take college courses while in high school. The plan was to earn my associate's, save my money, and move to LA. And if things didn't work out, I'd move back home and get my bachelor's. That was all my Virgo brain needed: a plan.

By the time senior year started, I was hyper-focused. Having completed most of my high school credits, I worked out a schedule that allowed me to stay in school for two hours and then go to Hillsborough Community College to take courses there. Around this time, a dance mom hired me to pick up her kids from school. So after my last class at about 2 p.m., I'd drive to an elementary school not too far away and wait for her children to be released: a five-year-old girl from one of my dance classes and her older brother. I'd either take them to the dance studio or drop them off at their grandma's.

After taxiing the kids around, I taught dance classes from 5 p.m. to 8 p.m., Monday to Thursday, for thirty dollars a class. Fridays and Saturdays were for solo, duet, and group rehearsals. For each solo, I earned $250 for choreography and had four rehearsals to teach the routine. If a student wanted more practice, each additional rehearsal cost thirty dollars per hour. Group rehearsals ranged from $300 to $450. Choreography pay was fruitful but only came around once a year before competition season. On Fridays and Saturdays—and on Sundays during holiday weekends—I go-go danced at local bars from 10 p.m. to 3 a.m., making a base rate of $100 plus tips, which ranged anywhere from $50 to $150.

Every Friday and Saturday for about two consecutive weeks, an older lesbian woman dressed in an oversized suit and a laid bob visited the clubs I worked at. She reminded me of Katt Williams, so we'll call her Miss Katt. Every night, Miss Katt sat in the corner of the club about six feet from my platform. The first night, her presence concerned me. She stared with intense, unwavering eye contact. If the club owner or other club patrons spoke to me, she sized them up as if they had to go through her first. After about an hour, I was ready to make a complaint with the head bouncer, but then the unthinkable happened: Miss

Katt dug into her pocket, pulled out a wad of money, and made it rain all over me! A mix of ones, fives, and twenties poured everywhere, a refreshing change from the usual two or three dollars the other patrons tipped. At the end of the night, I counted $275 in tips, most of which had come from Miss Katt.

For the most part, she was respectful and kept her distance. But one night Miss Katt got a little too loose.

Most nights, I never saw her drink. She might have taken a few puffs of a Black & Mild, but that was it. This night was different. Every time the shot o'clock horn rang through the club, she ordered a double. In between shots, a cup of dark liquor was glued to her hand. She tipped me abundantly, as usual, but this time she threw the money over me, happy-danced for the remainder of the song, and for the big finale, reached for my hips and dragged me off the platform. We landed in a jumbled mess on the floor. The squeal that left my mouth alerted the bouncer, who immediately started roughing up Miss Katt, and from that night on she was banned from the club. Over the two short weeks she'd been there, I made nine hundred dollars in tips.

I was grinding. Only three words can describe that time in my life: tired, overworked, and coffee-addicted. But at the same time, I was overwhelmed with hope. I could see my goals so clearly.

By the time I graduated, I'd passed five dual-enrollment courses, bringing me one step closer to an associate's degree. My tunnel vision was so narrow that I got cheap. I decided that nothing would affect my LA funds, so I didn't walk in my graduation. With a smile on my face, I requested for my diploma to arrive in the mail. I couldn't imagine spending ninety dollars on a cap and gown. Mami tried to convince me otherwise, desperately wishing that I would celebrate my 5.5 GPA, but I didn't want to spend an extra dime on anything. I also didn't go to prom.

After my last class on weekdays, I'd invite freestylers to dance with me at the studio, thus birthing my love for freestyle and later encouraging me to join my first dance crew. The studio owner, who was also my boss, fully supported my dreams and trusted me to close the studio after late-night training sessions. Some nights we wouldn't tire out until 2 a.m. Then I'd go to bed, wake up at 6 a.m., and do it all over again.

After high school, I attended Hillsborough Community College from 8 a.m. to 12 p.m. My routine stayed the same except for one new addition to my grind: applying for FAFSA, or federal student aid. It practically made my hair fall out. The multiple-page application asked questions only Mami could answer, but when I brought them to her, she seemed more confused than me! With some help from my older sister, I completed the task, and not only did I receive funding for my courses, but I had leftover grant money at the end of the semester—a financial aid refund that they politely added to a debit card. These leftover funds were meant to help with school supplies and room and board, but I lived at home and purchased used textbooks at quite the discount. So by the end of the semester, I had a whopping fifteen hundred dollars on my card.

After discovering the beauty that is the financial aid refund in my first semester of college, my plans changed. I decided to stay for two more semesters and then just do it. Go for it. Buy a flight and move to LA. A group of my friends had just made the leap, so I'd have a place to stay until I could get an apartment of my own. And with that, I made up my mind: after two semesters, I'd be on my way to La-La Land.

I came to grips with the fact that I wouldn't be getting my associate's after all, and I made a pact with myself that the rest of college wouldn't be stressful. I would learn what I wanted to and enroll in whatever classes my heart desired, whether they were on the associate's track or not. But stress-free wasn't the word; I had the time of my life. I filled my schedule with all the social science and English courses I could find: psychology, sociology, intro to child psych, creative writing, and world religion, just to name a few. I was tapped in, hungry for knowledge, and thoroughly enjoying my time. I attended college for three semesters total and added each financial aid refund to my moving fund.

In the fall, the popular competition show *So You Think You Can Dance*, also called *SYTYCD*, released its audition dates. The Los Angeles audition fell directly on my spring break, and that was all I needed to know. I went into plan-making overdrive. I bought a flight, solidified my housing, and researched classes to take while I was there. The audition only lasted one day, so I figured I should dip a toe into the city I'd be moving to that summer. I'd visited Los Angeles the year before for *SYTYCD* Finals Week, but we had stayed in Pasadena, and on the first round of cuts, I was on the chopping block. I was only there for forty-eight hours. This time, I would make the trip count.

And I guess I did, 'cause not only did I make it into the show's Top 20, but I met the woman who would become my best friend and future wife.

6
spring break

The days leading up to the audition were a wild ride. I got lost on the city bus three times, took a lot of terrible classes, and my hundred-dollar, forty-five-minute Uber from LAX to San Fernando Valley nearly sent me into a state of shock. I'm from a city you can tour in twenty minutes, or twenty-five if traffic is heavy that day. So bumper-to-bumper standstill traffic on the 405 appalled me.

Instagram led me to believe that teaching a class in LA was a privilege, something awarded to talented and highly revered instructors. After all, this was a major hub for the industry. I had no clue that there were still different levels of instructors, from beginner to advanced, no different than a lot of the open classes in Florida. I didn't know people could just rent a studio for an hour and teach a class. Surely they had to be professional choreographers, right? Otherwise, how could they just get up and teach a class in my dream city?

Boy, was I wrong. Most of the classes I attended that week were complete flops, movement-filled hours spent wondering, *How the hell did I get here?* I even ended up in a heels class strutting to the harmonious sounds of "Barbie Girl" by Aqua, a song I'd loved as a kid but never imagined performing a sensual heels routine to. Let's just say it's best to thoroughly research classes before hopping in. Dear reader, don't be like me.

Not all of them were terrible, though. I took an amazing hip-hop foundations class, and the astounding talent in the room left me shaken and inspired. When two of the best dancers approached me after class to ask if I'd like to head back to their garage studio to session, I was thrilled. An opportunity to session with amazing male freestylers, who somehow saw talent in my skillset too? Count me in!

An hour later, as I was freestyling and exploring movement, it became evident that these two dancers wanted to explore my personal life instead. They danced very little and asked tons of questions about my love life and whether I was in a relationship. When I realized why they'd actually invited me, I left.

That situation hadn't bothered me too much, though. I was more upset that I'd been fooled in the same way before. They'd seen me, a cute girl hoping to improve her skills in freestyling, asked to session, and seized the opportunity for other reasons.

Thankfully, none of these experiences ended in assault, but they did affect me emotionally. To this day, I second-guess praise from men in the dance community. Every time I receive a compliment from a man, I rush through a sea of thoughts: *What kind of outfit do I have on? Some of the styles I do are more sensual than others—what type of movement was I doing at that moment? Does he know I'm married to a woman? Is he the kind of man to disregard my union because we're both women?*

Those first days in LA were strange, to say the least.

The audition process for *SYTYCD* was an all-day excursion. Before the on-stage audition that America saws, there were two untelevised rounds in front of the producers. These auditions were a free-for-all. You had thirty seconds, if you were lucky, to go out there and give it your all, no matter what corny song they decided to play. I didn't understand this yet, but competitive television shows—especially the types that teeter into reality TV, like *SYTYCD*—search for all kinds of traits in their contestants. Sometimes sheer talent isn't enough. So when I witnessed amazing dancers get cut ten seconds into their auditions, I couldn't understand why. I also didn't have time to panic, so I reeled it in and focused on calming my spiking anxiety.

By the grace of God, I made it through all three auditions. The judges showcased nothing but love and admiration for my style of dance, and I was on cloud nine! It was the perfect end to my spring break. Excitement rushed through my veins, but fatigue crept around the corner. My day began at 7 a.m. as I waited to enter the theater. I got in at around 10 a.m. and finished my auditions by 3 p.m. The day wasn't over, though. Once the audition process ended, the showrunners lumped us into groups of ten or fifteen and sent us to different parts of production: interviews, media shoots, behind-the-scenes footage, background checks—you name it!

They herded us around in groups, but each dancer completed each station alone, leaving the rest of us bored to tears in the lobby while we waited. So what did a group of strangers from all over do? We spoke to each other to pass the time. I can't tell you who else was in my group because the moment they sectioned us off, I hit it off with somebody. She went by SHEstreet then, which was a shortened version of her name, Sheopatra Streeter. Not only was she bright and outgoing, but she was also a phenomenal dancer. One of the greatest I'd ever seen.

I was six months into my transition from studio styles to street styles of dance, and by the looks of SHE, she'd been in the game for years. She moved with a seasoned precision that outmatched a lot of the men that day. Women weren't exactly saturating the Central Florida freestyle community back then, so I'd grown accustomed to being outnumbered and outskilled. But from the moment I met her, though it would take me years to notice, SHE single-handedly began undoing those norms for me.

7
vegas week

S tress, stress, and more stress, sprinkled with a dash of
sleep deprivation—those are the words I'd use to describe
the *SYTYCD* Finals Week in Las Vegas, Nevada. In total, 150
dancers made it through the nationwide audition, and now it
was time to make more cuts. By the end of the week, the judges
would select their Top 20: the group that would go on to make
the official TV show.

For the first round, contestants had to perform solos for the
judges again, perhaps to remind them why we deserved to be in
Vegas in the first place. For my audition the previous year, the
first round was hip-hop choreography, which I got cut from in
the blink of an eye, so this time I was ready to give it my all. To
go harder than I did last time. A mantra played in my head: *You
don't have to make it all the way to the end. Just get a little further
than you did last time.*

During my solo performance, the audience and the judges responded positively. But when I look back at that footage now, I can't help but cringe a little. I'm a completely different dancer now. I've grown light-years since then, but I'm grateful 'cause my talent still got me through doors. I made it past the first round with rave reviews from the judges.

From then on, I felt like I was in a blender, a spinning funnel filled with different challenges and more cuts. The theme for my season of *SYTYCD* was Stage Vs. Street, a head-to-head competition that pitted the technical styles of dance—like ballet, jazz, contemporary, and ballroom—against the street styles, such as popping, hip-hop, freestyle, break-dancing, and krumping. I'd grown up training in predominately technical styles, but when I turned eighteen, things changed. The freestyle community in Central Florida inspired me. Their seemingly endless supply of moves baffled me, as if movement just seeped from their bodies. I was groomed in a world where every single step was handed to us. Every kick, turn, and leap was choreographed. The street community didn't have anything handed to them. It was all straight off the dome, from their brain to their limbs. No dance teacher spoon-fed the steps to them.

Nowadays, referring to hip-hop styles as "street styles" rubs me the wrong way. It perpetuates the idea that these styles lack structure, foundation, and prestige just because they were born from street culture. The instructors at my performing arts high school shared this sentiment. For the longest, the owner of my childhood dance studio refused to integrate hip-hop classes into her school because she didn't want her students "booty dancing." Referring to this art as a "street style" negates the fact that it is an art—an art that has changed the world and the people who practice it. From almost every city with a large population of African Americans, a dance was born. Memphis Jookin, Chicago Footwork, Detroit Jit—the list goes on. This phenomenon is identical to the different dances cultivated in tribes all over Africa. It's black American folklore and should be revered as such.

Before I transitioned to hip-hop styles, improvising to anything except soft instrumental music scared me senseless. Me, keeping up with syncopated trap drums and funky bass lines? Never. But after a while, in good ol' Yoe (or Virgo) fashion, I wanted to stop being scared. I wanted to get rid of that fear in the pit of my stomach every time I tried to freestyle, so I began training and never looked back. Eight months later, when the SYTYCD auditions rolled around, I had to choose: Street or Stage? Though I grew up on the stage side, I'd spent almost a year diving headfirst into an exciting new world. A world that had revived my love and passion for dance in ways I can't even describe. A world that I didn't see myself leaving anytime soon. So when I got to the front of that audition line in LA and the producer asked, "Team Street or Team Stage?", I chose Street.

I connected with the artists in that room. Together we mourned every round of cuts. I'll never forget the gasps that echoed through the audience when Angyil, one of the most amazing movement artists in the world, got cut. Though people had always told me it wasn't just about dance, that was the moment I truly understood how other powers influenced these choices.

The competition kept us up at all hours of the night. One night we ended so late that I only had an hour to sleep before the next day began. My body was so sore afterward that taking a bath became my priority. A five-to-ten-minute soak followed by a quick cat nap—that had been the plan. However, I woke up startled by my alarm clock and sitting in cold water. I'd dozed off in the tub!

I have a theory that the show did this on purpose. On those sleep-deprived days toward the end of the week, cameras popped up more often than usual, appearing at the slightest whiff of disarray.

During the group choreography round, we were split into teams of five and given one night to choreograph a two-minute piece. (Hence, why I ended up falling asleep in my tub later.) One particular group member was extremely difficult; we'll call him Ted. Everyone did their best to remain as goal-oriented and efficient as possible while choreographing a piece that show-cased each artist in a good light, aiming to finish in time to get some rest. But Ted wasn't having any of it. He shot down almost every idea we put out there, replacing them with larger-than-life suggestions that would need way more than one night of rehearsal to flesh out.

The producers sensed the tension from miles away, so they did what they do best: stirred the pot. For the most part, we did an astounding job at keeping our cool, but from time to time one of us released a long sigh or rolled our eyes. And the moment we expressed a hint of strain, the cameras and interviews rolled in, adding more interruptions to our rehearsal.

"So how's working with the group?" one of the producers asked after pulling me aside for an interview in the middle of our already short rehearsal.

"It's great!" I began, knowing exactly where he was headed. "We still have a few parts to iron out, but it's getting there."

A slight smirk appeared in the corner of his mouth. "So, how's working with Ted?"

"Working with Ted has been a show in itself! He's charismatic and has so many ideas."

I wasn't completely lying. Ted *was* charismatic and had an endless well of ideas. Were they conducive to the team as a whole? No, not really, but I politely left that thought out. I refused to feed into the drama they were trying to brew. We had enough on our plates.

I found solace in hanging out with Sheopatra. In between rounds of cuts and at meal breaks, I talked with her about anything and everything. At the time, we were both in relationships, so these were solely platonic feelings. But I was sure of one thing: I'd be leaving this experience with a new friend.

8

celebrities are weirdos

Dragging one foot in front of the other and carrying two oversized duffel bags on my shoulders, I sluggishly exited the arena. I was on the *So You Think You Can Dance* Tour, performing somewhere down south in a city I can't remember. Following the show, we showered in the arena, packed our bags, and made our way to the tour buses where we'd eat after-show food, climb into our bunks, and travel to the next city while we slept. When my eyes opened the next morning or afternoon, I'd be in a different city, at a different arena, preparing for yet another show.

On most tours, we're scheduled for a couple of nights of shows followed by an off day. The number of shows will vary from job to job. For this particular tour, we were performing seventy shows over the course of four months, with a three-to-one week (three shows and an off day) or a four-to-one week (four shows and an off day). It was only day two of a four-show week, and I was already exhausted.

The second show was done, and two more were left. In two days my limbs would be swallowed by a plush hotel bed and my skin would be basking in a bath rather than the communal showers offered by arenas.

Two more days, I reassured myself. *Two more days and about ten more feet until I reach the tour bus, and then I'll be able to sit back and rel—*

"OMG!!! It's her!"

As soon as I turned the corner, I saw a sea of about thirty fans crowded between the tour bus and my body like a human barricade.

"Ahhh! Yorelis! You were amazing! Can I get a picture?!"

I inhaled and exhaled. Thirty fans, pictures, and autographs —that would take about an hour. That meant an hour before after-show food would reach my belly and Lord knows how long till sleep. Not to mention that I'd be lugging two duffel bags full of show gear from fan to fan. A few pictures and autographs shouldn't take too long in theory, but I had to leave room for conversation about everything under the sun.

So there I was, fifteen minutes into a story told by a mother whose three-year-old daughter wanted to be just like me when she grew up. The toddler was shy, not saying more than a meek "hi," but I engaged as much as I could.

After excusing myself at the politest conversational break, I ended up with another fan a few feet over—an older white woman who insisted on showing me twenty pictures of her gorgeous grandbabies because "they looked just like" me. By the fourth picture, it was evident that their caramel-drop faces did not resemble mine. Their greenish-hazel eyes were nowhere near the hue of my dark brown. Tight, blond curls spiraled wildly from their scalps while my curls were dark brown. But they were some of the cutest babies I'd ever laid eyes on. After she showed me the photos, I asked if she had any videos. Before I knew it, I was watching chunky baby thighs waddle across her phone screen and listening to infectious baby giggles. They didn't look like me in the slightest. Perhaps she just thought that because the babies were mixed race, like me.

As I inched closer and closer to the bus, I posed for a few more pictures and scribbled a couple of autographs. The last fan was a teenage girl who aspired to be a professional dancer.

"I turn eighteen in two years and I want nothing more than to audition for *So You Think You Can Dance*. Do you have any advice for me?" she asked.

Hm, I thought. *Have a therapist on speed dial? Work on public speaking so you don't professionally fumble through interviews like I do? Keep the fridge heavily stocked with wine? Prayer, prayer, and more prayer?*

I smiled and took a breath. "Work really hard over the next two years. Try dabbling in dance styles you've never tried before. If it doesn't work out the first time, don't let that discourage you from trying again."

Her eyes lit up, and a smile spread from ear to ear. "Thank you so much!"

That was it. The last person to talk to. Nothing stood between me and my home on wheels but a metal barricade and a security guard. I flashed my credential and took a step forward when out of nowhere, a large hand grabbed my shoulder from behind and tugged me backward. The weight of the duffel bags combined with the force of the pull sent me stumbling back.

What the hell?

As I found my balance, my eyes followed the heavy hand to the body it was attached to: a middle-aged woman surrounded by four little girls.

"Yorelis!" she yelled. "You just *have* to take a picture with my students! They just absolutely *adore* you!"

I adjusted my face, which was still contorted from a stranger putting her hand on me and nearly dragging me to the pavement.

"Yeah, we can take a picture," I replied, despite her request being a demand rather than a question.

After plastering a smile on my face for a few more seconds, I practically ran onto the bus.

I'd never really thought about the life of a celebrity before. If thoughts did come to mind, they were nothing short of awe and admiration. By that time, I'd never met a celebrity or even attended a concert. I didn't know what it was like to see someone outside of a TV screen and be unable to contain myself. But I would never, ever, put my hands on someone. I would never demand a photo. And I would never tug at someone from behind.

It's impossible to know how someone will react to something like that. In high school I was jumped by a group of girls. The ordeal began when a classmate forcibly tugged at my shoulder from behind, just like that woman had done. What if PTSD had taken over, forcing me to react with profanity and flying fists? Or what if I hadn't regained my balance when I fell backward? I could've been hurt. Overall, I was flabbergasted by her blatant disregard for my body, but I still wasn't comfortable addressing it.

I have a fan base that includes a devoted group of social media followers. I don't consider myself a celebrity, but *SYTYCD* revealed a piece of that world to me. A world where it didn't matter if I was tired, hungry, or lugging two jumbo-sized duffel bags in my arms—I still belonged to the fans. If I didn't prioritize the fans, I risked being labeled as stuck-up or rude.

For the most part, celebrities aren't weirdos; they're regular human beings like you and me. It's just hard for them to be regular because of the permanent microscope they reside under. If I'm exhausted or in a bad mood, it doesn't take much to float through the day silent and unapproachable. Besides the random man who takes it upon himself to let me know I should "smile more," no one is really bothered by my chosen temperament for the day. I have the liberty to leave my house in an oversized t-shirt, sunglasses, and sweats, and social media won't see my exquisite home wear if I don't want them to.

If a celebrity does the same, they'll say she must be hiding a pregnancy or weight gain under that oversized t-shirt. If deemed unapproachable that day, he might be labeled as rude. Celebrities aren't allowed the same off days. While vacationing with their families in a crowded resort, they have to choose between spending quality time with loved ones or posing for fan pictures out of the blue. Something as simple as a sunburn, relaxed belly, or unruly beach hair is like gold to tabloids.

When I used to think about celebrities, I figured it must be tiresome to have cameras trailing them all the time, but that was about it. Otherwise, I really couldn't care less. They're rich and famous; so what if they can't take a walk without people recognizing them? They'll be fine!

The *SYTYCD* Tour gave me a taste of physical celebrity life: screaming fans, pictures, and so many autographs. The *SYTYCD* television show granted me a glimpse into celebrity social media life.

Seconds after the show announced the Top 20 Dancers, my following on Instagram and Twitter broke through the ceiling. My one thousand followers rose to forty thousand by the end of the week.

If I had to use one word to describe my followers during this stage of my life, I'd call them *interesting*. While watching any reality TV show, we all subconsciously scan through the participants: Who's the most relatable? Who's the most beautiful? Who has the most aggravating personality? Back in the day, while watching *Bad Girls Club* or *Flavor of Love*, my friends and I engaged in detailed discussions about our favorite and least favorite people. We gossiped, laughed, and predicted upcoming drama, but that was it. We didn't waste too much time talking about these people we didn't know at all. Reaching out to them via Myspace or Facebook wasn't even a thought in our heads.

Those same discussions I'd had about TV personalities back in the day were now being had about me, thanks to the wonderful world of social media.

The majority of my traffic was love and admiration:

"I love your dancing!"

"Your movement is magical."

"You're so gorgeous!"

A lot of the dialogue was inquisitive:

"Where are you from?"

"What's your ethnicity?"

And then there was the other end of the stick—the downright nasty:

"Your dancing sucks."

"You aren't going to last long on the show."

And a personal favorite of mine, one I hadn't heard in a while:

"Ugly half-breed bitch."

My adolescence and early adulthood had its fair share of drama. Best-friend fallouts, cat fights, and everything under the sun. But nothing could've prepared me for internet trolls and the never-ending phone notifications pinging every two minutes. After the initial shock, I leapt into self-preservation mode. With the goal of protecting my mental health at all costs, I created three rules:

1. control the amount of time spent on social media.

This prevented me from becoming fixated on positive or negative attention. I'd read, scroll, take it for what it was, and then sign out and go on with the rest of my day. This rule also helped me be present during this once-in-a-lifetime experience.

2. don't reply to negative comments.

Trolls don't want to discuss. They want drama. They want attention. My sanity wasn't worth it.

3. post and then get out of there.

In the past, I would refresh my page as the comments rolled in. Because of all the different types of comments, my emotions would rise, fall, and spin around like they were on a wild theme-park ride. Now, I was choosing not to get on the ride at all.

After much trial and error, I started to find the middle ground. The trolls weren't affecting me as much as they had in the past, but other aspects of social media began to take their toll.

Many celebrities lead multifaceted lives; most people do. A

woman might be famous for causing an immature ruckus on reality TV, but she may also be a phenomenal engineer. As shocking as it may be, many rappers are college educated, despite their vulgarity or crude lyrics. Some of the most Bible-loving older black women I know will still curse like a sailor if you do them wrong, but that doesn't eliminate their love for God. Ebonics, profanity, and tattoos are not indicators of intelligence in the least bit. I'm saying all of this with confidence now, but it took me years to learn.

When Colin Kaepernick kneeled in protest of police brutality, I was perturbed to see how many fans commented phrases like "Less thinking, more playing!" or "Just play football!" As if Kaepernick didn't deserve to express his beliefs. Football was his talent, the only thing he was good for, the only thing people cared to see. Same with me. My followers weren't interested in posts about my family, friends, or other interests. If it wasn't related to dance or *So You Think You Can Dance*, it didn't receive traction.

I felt like I had to clean up my language. I couldn't let words like "ain't" and "finna" leave my mouth during an interview because I thought people would see me as uneducated or ghetto. Twangs in my accent, such as "cain't" instead of "can't," had to be polished as well. I couldn't be the boisterous, around-the-way Florida girl; poised Disney star was the mold. Because of these rampant thoughts, most of my interviews were a jittery, stutter-filled mess.

I always had to be on. My posts had to radiate success, talent, and happiness, with no room for actual human emotion. I didn't dare tell fans how tired I was from a twelve-hour rehearsal or that I was losing way too much weight, probably due to stress. Despite my frustration, I could never vent about the excessive heat damage my hair was experiencing at the hands of the terrible hair team. Nope. The only emotion I could evoke was "I'm so happy to be here." And I was. I was more than thankful to be given such a big opportunity. But my physical, spiritual, and mental health were shaken around like forks in the garbage disposal.

About four weeks into the show, I was eliminated. After the competition was over, the network took the Top 10 Dancers and two alternates on a national tour where they would perform memorable routines from the show. I was blessed to have been chosen as an alternate. This is when my relationship with social media began to shift. Less pressure weighed on my shoulders. My posts reflected more than just a dancing robot. Light curse words, such as "damn" or "ass," appeared in my captions. Yoe the human started to peek through. I liked human Yoe, and so did my fans.

That was short-lived.

"You're gay?! Wow, I'm so disappointed…"

"Racism doesn't exist. Stop promoting it."

"A gay person could never win *SYTYCD*. No wonder you were eliminated." Despite the show having its fair share of queer winners.

Those were just a few of the loving messages I received.

You see, after the show ended, my uptightness around social media began to loosen more by the day. Three months later, I felt fully unraveled. I debuted videos of nights at gay bars in different cities on my Instagram and Twitter. I added heart-eye emojis to pictures of beautiful women on my stories. As videos of police brutality went viral, I reposted them with a vengeance. I vocalized my opinions on racist white America and posted sources to back up my thoughts. The needs of my followers floated out of my mind. I was taking back my social media for personal use. The plastic, unrealistic, "happy to be here" Yoe was on her way out. She would be replaced with a real human with real emotions, beliefs, and standards.

The thousands of followers I'd gained from *SYTYCD*, which were predominately middle-aged, conservative white Americans, were not happy. Actually, they were livid. How dare the sweet, talented person they fell in love with on TV go against most of their beliefs! How dare she be pro-choice, support true racial equality, and date women! It was too much for them to handle, and they didn't waste any chance to let me know.

At first, the influx of hate hit me hard. I couldn't fathom why people were so comfortable messaging a stranger such rude things. Having come out at fifteen, I'd almost forgotten how strongly people felt about my sexual orientation. Why were they so angry about whom I chose to lie with at the end of the day, something they'd never have to see?

These messages sent me through an array of emotions, but in hindsight I'm grateful for the process. I was able to shed so many unsupportive followers on social media during that time. By consistently staying true to myself and blocking a few profiles, the negativity cleared and positivity took its place, as well as a large amount of empathy and patience. Now my followers are loving and inclusive critical thinkers. I can post a picture of my wife doing a cartwheel, and it'll receive as much love as a makeup-saturated selfie. From my brand to my artistry, from my activism to my writing, they support it all, and I appreciate them every day for it.

9

my firsts

Getting started in the industry looks different for everyone. Some dancers join a training program offered by a choreographer they'd like to work with. Others serially audition until they land a job. Some spend years just trying to get signed. I've seen dancers book work solely from their social media accounts, without an agent or audition in sight. There's no black-and-white way to book jobs. It's different for everyone.

Some say that success is a mix of luck, opportunity, and talent. I'm blessed to say that my start in the industry was exactly that. Luck was on my side when I was selected to be a contestant on *SYTYCD*.

Competition shows can be a toss-up. Sometimes the winner takes off running and goes on to become a household name, booking commercials and tours and teaching at all the major conventions. Other times, the winner fades back into normal society, auditioning and dreaming just like the rest of the dance community. Sometimes a dancer doesn't even have to win the show to become a household name.

My run on the show was cut short after I was eliminated at the Top 14. The fans I gained from the show were loving for the most part, but a lot of them ran to the unfollow button once I began posting about my queer lifestyle.

My string of *SYTYCD* luck continued with Reina Hidalgo, a choreographer I had the pleasure of working with on the show. After making the move to LA and being exposed to different types of people from all over, I started to miss home: Caribbean accents filling my ears, smells from my favorite cultural foods swirling about my nostrils, Latino music pulsating through my body. When I met Reina, a black Cuban woman from South Florida, she felt like an oasis in the desert.

From her clothes to her accent, she warmed a part of my heart that had cooled since my move. Even the unapologetic Cuban profanities that slipped from her mouth brought a smile to my face. She was the perfect medicine for a young, hardly adult woman far away from home and navigating a national television show.

Time was always limited. Because new episodes aired every Monday, we were left with six days to learn and rehearse multiple dance routines. Though this limitation threatened to loom over the creative process like a dark cloud, Reina never allowed it. Before each rehearsal, she'd pull us into a circle for meditation and breathing exercises. She spoke life into us during a time when it seemed like our destinies belonged to American voters.

Basically, Reina was the shit. In the privacy of close friends, I even deemed Reina my Cuban madrina—my godmother.

Somehow, someway, I made an impression on her too. Months after the show, we were preparing for the *SYTYCD* Tour where we'd be performing viewers' favorite routines from the show in live theaters across the nation.

"Hey, are you going back to Florida or LA after the tour?" Gabi asked. She and Reina knew each other from Miami.

"I'm going back to LA. I'll finally get settled, then let my agents know I'm ready to start auditioning. Hopefully book something."

"Reina wants to know if we'll be available to work on this TV show she's choreographing on in February."

Our tour was over at the end of January, so the stars had aligned perfectly.

"Really?! Okay! Let her know I won't be going back to Florida. I'll be in LA."

"All right, she said she'll reach out closer to the date."

During the rehearsal process, I received a call from Reina. And that's how I got my first job, dancing on a Hulu series called *East Los High*. I was part of a dance crew called Jefferson Park, the enemy team to East Los. Our captain was the antagonist to one of the main characters. After shooting a couple of episodes, the writers introduced a new character named Baby Girl, a dancer on Jefferson Park's crew. She was full of life and ready to mouth off to anyone who looked at her too long. The director opened auditions to me and a few other dancers, and I booked the role. On a multiple-episode SAG TV show, I was dancing *and* acting. Once again, I was on cloud nine. I was a Los Angeles transplant whose biggest fear was moving back to Florida with her tail between her legs because she'd blown through her savings and couldn't book a job. It took years for that fear to subside, but *East Los* helped alleviate the stress for a few weeks. All because of Reina Hidalgo.

While I was on the show, I met Adrian Thompkins, one of my fellow members on Jefferson Park's dance team. Over the weeks of shooting, we had a few laughs in rehearsal and during long days on set. Since he's originally from Houston, we shared sentiments about how much we missed the South. He even gave me a ride from rehearsal a couple of times. I loved our conversations, but I wouldn't say we were the best of friends. So when Adrian reached out to me weeks after wrapping our last episode of *East Los High*, I was shocked.

"Hey, are you a SAG member?" he inquired.

"Yeah, I joined this year," I said, shuddering at the memory of paying three thousand dollars to join the Screen Actors Guild union.

"Perfect. Are you available tomorrow and three days after that?"

"Yeah."

And just like that, I ended up on the set of my first music video, "Superlove" by Tinashe, recommended by Adrian and under the direction of JaQuel Knight.

If you ask my wife, she'll say I landed in LA, booked my first job, and haven't stopped working since. If you ask me, I worked a lot but also experienced a few dry spells. And even when work was great, I still broke several sweats waiting for checks to arrive in the mail—a feeling that always tickled my fear of moving back home.

My LA origin story is rare; my talent met opportunity and good timing. That's nowhere near the case for most dancers. Sometimes it takes months to get signed, more months to get an audition email from your agent, and even longer to book a job. And in addition to having your fate tossed in the air, your friends and family will be calling from back home, asking, "So did you work with any famous people yet?"

————

My first years on Instagram were like most people's. I had about a thousand followers, mainly from my school and dance life. I posted pictures of anything and everything. I posted a lot of videos, but their quality was only as good as my camcorder and ancient iPhone could provide. These fifteen-second clips—that's all Instagram allowed at the time—were of me dancing barefoot in an empty parking lot, dance studio, or grassy field, to tracks by a band called the Local Natives. I was the epitome of a contemporary dancer.

My first jump in followers came from the Central Florida freestyle community. There aren't too many dancers in that community compared to big cities like LA and New York, and at that time I could probably count the number of female dancers on one hand. So when I entered the freestyle scene, I received a lot of attention despite my lack of skill, thus birthing my first big spike of fifty to seventy-five new followers. Though they were spread between Facebook and Instagram, the heavy influx of new likes stunned me.

Some might not consider that many followers to be much of an influx, but to this Tampa girl, it felt like I was in the popular club. People expressed their love and support for my dancing, which meant everything during my transition from studio dancer to freestyler.

But nothing could've prepared me to jump from one thousand to forty thousand followers after the first episode of *SYTYCD* aired. Everything—comments, likes, fan mail, hate mail—rushed into my life like a tsunami. It forced me to get a grip, quickly. I decided not to let the likes go to my head; I could always find ways to improve as a dancer. I tried to ignore the hate, delete, block, and move on, but that rule was hard to follow sometimes.

———

After getting eliminated from *SYTYCD*, I started to disconnect my social media presence from the naive girl who was trying to win a competition show on FOX. Once I'd unraveled that character, another one appeared: Yorelis, a nineteen-year-old woman who sometimes dances to explicit music, who twerks EVERY TIME "Back That Azz Up" comes on, and who—oh, yeah—likes women. I revealed this character—the *real* me—monumentally slowly, taking deep breaths before hitting the post button and scrolling past the hateful messages in my inbox. I didn't dive in yelling, "Hey! This is the real me, bitches!" It was a slow transition, like a flower blooming after a long winter. This was my first real introduction to all the new followers I had acquired.

Though the revelation was slow, the reaction was not. Thousands of people unfollowed me at the speed of light. Most didn't leave quietly either; they left a hurtful comment or DM on their way out. After losing about twenty thousand followers, I started over again, rebuilding the Instagram I'd harbored such a love–hate relationship for.

two tips as you wait for your firsts in la:

- Be patient. There might be a lot of no's, and a lot of things won't go the way you intended. But the ratio of no's to yes's doesn't matter. What matters is that one *yes* that creates the snowball effect.
- There's a first for everything, but firsts aren't always glitter and rainbows. Accept them as they come and learn the lessons they provide.

10
detective work

B ecause we're artists, because we love our craft, because this joy keeps us young at heart, "young" energy runs rampant through us, circulating through our bodies and souls. We're very personable. Our body is our tool, so we're always active. We're energetic, youthful, and maybe a little crazy for choosing such an abnormal career.

This energy that does so much good for us can also turn south. Sometimes the atmosphere in this industry feels *too* youthful, almost adolescent. People talk behind other people's backs, spread rumors, and date within our small community.

If I've learned one thing, it's that people talk. A LOT.

I've heard stories about the same choreographer from different people who aren't connected to one another. I've asked dancers, "So how was that clothing campaign?" And every response was either a sigh of disbelief because of the horrible treatment they'd endured, or a sigh of relief because the trauma was over.

Many of the stories that spread like wildfire are about relationships. Like when two dancers are getting intimate on tour, but the rest of the crew knows about the guy's girlfriend back in LA. I've seen situations like this too many times to count. If I'm not close with the male dancer, I just look the other way, mind my business, and avoid his girlfriend when she visits him on the road. It never feels good to see a male dancer flaunting his girlfriend for a few days when the cast knows he's been cheating on her the whole time. But hey, it's not my business.

This isn't to raise your anxiety if you're dating a dancer in the industry. I also don't want to act like male dancers are the only ones to cheat while on the road. I know a female dancer who started a whole relationship with a woman on tour and then returned home to normal business with her husband. After a few months, she introduced the idea of exploring polyamory and adding a third to their relationship. Then bingo! She had the perfect first contender: her coworker from the tour.

For one tour, we were in New York for about a week, which is almost unheard of. I'm accustomed to finishing a show, showering, falling asleep on the tour bus, and waking up in a new city the next day to repeat the process. But then the unpredictable occurred: New York for a *week*. Seven days of tasty food, amazing nightlife after our shows, and even better shopping.

I was so excited to be stationary for such a long time that I flew my wife out to spend the week with me. As soon as she landed, we fell into a routine; we'd wake up, explore the city, eat some yummy food, and return to the hotel in time for me to shower and get ready for the show that night.

One day we strolled into the hotel lobby, stomachs full and Forever 21 bags in our hands, when we ran into Regina.

"Ooo, guys, I gotta tell y'all something!"

She pulled us into the corner behind a fake tree. Not suspicious at all. Instantly assuming her news was tea, SHE and I lowered our heads toward Regina.

"What's going on?" I asked.

She giggled sheepishly and looked around. "I think Terell has a girl locked in his room!"

"What?!" we said in unison.

"No, no, no, not like that. There's this girl I follow on Instagram, @lovelucy. I've been peeping her and Terell's online flirting for a minute now. He likes her pictures, she likes his. He comments heart eyes, so does she. So I looked at her Instagram story today, and she posted all these videos and pictures in *this* hotel!"

Regina was known for her ability to sniff out some tea. From pre-confirmed tour announcements to tourmances (tour romances), Regina always knew about it first.

"This hotel?!" we said like identical twins, yet again.

"Yes! Look!"

The décor in our hotel was eccentric: abstract paintings in the rooms and restrooms, oddly shaped asymmetrical windows. And in typical New York fashion, the rooms were tiny. I looked down at Regina's phone screen. It displayed a pretty white girl with wavey dirty-blonde hair, green eyes, and all those hotel details sprinkled in the background of her Instagram content.

A video of her jumping on the hotel bed while abstract paintings sat like flies on the wall.

A selfie with an asymmetrical window peeking out from behind her.

The same tiny, overpriced layout as our hotel room posing as the backdrop in all her content.

My tongue almost dried out due to how long my jaw remained open. SHE mirrored my expression.

"Has she been here the whole time?" I asked.

"Yes, she's one of my students. I watch her stories every day. She started posting herself in this hotel room a day before we got here."

"Wait, so how do you know she's here for Terell? Maybe she's here for something..." I trailed off, unable to believe my own attempt at playing devil's advocate.

"No, look at this post. You see that bag and that pair of shoes in the corner?"

There they were as plain as day: Terell's shoes with the same scuff marks he'd earned in rehearsals, and his infamous yellow book bag with patches all over.

"She's been here the whole time?! Just cooped up when we all go out after the shows?!" I asked.

"Girl, yes. Look at this clip."

Regina raised her phone again to reveal a video of @lovelucy in the hotel room at eleven last night—the same time the rest of the crew was at an after-party.

Giggles erupted from SHE's belly. "Damn, did sis ever leave?"

Regina and I couldn't help but laugh with her.

No one will ever know whether Terell had @lovelucy as a secret guest in his room that week, except for maybe his close friends. But if he did, Terell really managed shows, after-parties, and a hidden bae-cation. I applaud him. As a person who gets overwhelmed by going to the grocery store and the bank on the same day, that level of multitasking inspires me.

After witnessing Regina's detective work, I knew there was no way she was the only woman of her breed. Most women are intuitive by nature, so I worry for the men out there thinking about stepping toward the wild side. We're private investigators!

Later on, I heard other dancers who weren't on the tour discussing Terell's meeting with @lovelucy in New York. Dancers sure do talk. A LOT.

11

my first scam

I didn't have time for this. I HAD to get out of my current living situation. Not only did I live in a three-bedroom apartment with seven people, but one of those people was my ex. The ex-*boyfriend* I'd dated for a couple of months before I went on tour.

For this tour, we were housed in a hotel for rehearsals, probably because it was easier to bus us to and from work every day. We were assigned roommates, but I couldn't care less. One roommate beat six any day.

After my second week in the hotel, strange feelings bubbled inside of me. Rehearsals were long, lasting anywhere from eight to ten hours, but they didn't take up all of my time. Upon returning to the hotel, I ate dinner with my coworkers, visited the Jacuzzi, or read a book. I loved my free time after work. I craved that time to myself, and I cherished every second of it. However, uncertain feelings continued to brew within me.

At first, I couldn't pinpoint the source of these emotions, but by the end of week two, it was crystal clear: I hadn't called my boyfriend in almost two weeks.

After moving into the hotel, I answered very few of his texts and practically none of his calls. "I'm sorry. Rehearsal ran so late today. I'm probably gonna eat and go to sleep"—that was the message I sent out the most. He was always sweet and understanding, replying, "Okay I love you. Get some rest. Have a good night."

But the problem was, I texted nothing but lies. Rehearsals *did* run long sometimes, and I *was* exhausted. That much was true. But I always managed to stay up late reading, watching TV, or sessioning with my coworkers.

I started to feel crazy. Absolutely insane. Not because I hadn't spoken to him in two weeks, but because I didn't want to.

I didn't want to admit it yet, but those two weeks in the hotel, with a complete stranger as my roomie, felt like a vacation on a remote tropical island. A vacation from seven people sharing one bathroom. A vacation from an apartment with no central AC. And as much as I didn't want to admit it, a vacation from my boyfriend.

I didn't miss him, and it made me feel absolutely terrible. I should've missed him, right? That's how relationships work! In the past, I missed my ex-girlfriend all the time. Whether it was one week or one hour, I missed her with everything in me. But for some reason, I didn't miss my boyfriend. I didn't know why, but I knew I couldn't waste his time anymore. I couldn't drag him along any further. That wasn't fair. So, during the third week of rehearsals, right before the tour started, I invited him to my hotel to talk. He arrived with a smile from ear to ear, excited to see me after such a long time. And then I broke up with him.

Judging from his energy and the heart-tugging look on his face, I didn't break his heart—I shattered it into a million tiny pieces. It took a while to get that image of him out of my head, to shake the energy of that moment. The whole ordeal, breaking someone's heart, made me so sad, but I kept reminding myself of my feelings and the freeness I felt without him. Like a mantra, I repeatedly said to myself, *This is going to be better in the end. Don't drag it out for either of us.*

———

He took it well for the most part. By my second month on tour, he'd reached out a couple of times. Little texts here and there inquiring about the tour and my experience. I loved our communication. It felt like I was finally living a mature, adult dating life. Compared to the breakup with my ex-girlfriend, which ended in chaos, violence, and a no-contact separation, this was like night and day. He and I were texting and laughing, almost like the days when we were just friends. It was amazing. That is, until he found out I was getting to know Sheopatra more.

I spent the fourth and last month of the tour in some of the coldest places in North America. In January. The plummeting temperatures forced the Florida girl inside me to react accordingly. On our days off, I didn't leave my hotel AT ALL. I watched a lot of Netflix, had all my meals delivered, and started talking to SHE every day.

We'd spend hours on the phone as we caught each other up on life events. She poked fun at how I Facetimed her from different parts of my tiny hotel room, which was entirely true. Hour one started at the foot of my bed. By hour two, I'd be by the windowsill. Fast-forward to hour five, I'd be sitting in the bathtub, fully clothed, staring at the ceiling as we got to know each other at a level above friendship.

One night, after spending hours Facetiming SHE in my comfy hotel bed, I ran to the restroom. In good ol' Gen Z fashion (though I'm technically a millennial), I took my phone with me, propping it up so she could only see me from the shoulders up.

While I peed, a string of continual giggles came from her end.

"What?"

She was so caught up in whatever was tickling her that she ignored me.

"Ugh, seriously. What's so funny?" I repeated.

Before she could get a word out, my phone buzzed. A text message from her. It was a screenshot of me from the shoulders up, on the toilet, facing profile, with the back of my curly hair standing straight up as flat as a board. Clearly I'd been in bed sitting up against the wall for hours, because my hair had kept the shape of that wall despite my moving.

That picture ignited our funny bones to no end. We laughed, changed the subject, then circled back to laugh some more. My flat wall hair was so funny, I posted the screenshot on Twitter.

The humor must've resonated with others 'cause it received quite a few likes.

A couple of hours later, I received a text from one of my roommates in LA.

> Hey, idk what happened, but Fulano put all your stuff out y'all's bedroom and into the middle of the living room.

All my stuff. The stuff he'd let me keep in his room since I didn't have time to move it before the tour.

My ex-boyfriend saw none of the humor in that picture. His eyes probably shot right past my wall hair, straight toward who I was Facetiming and the time stamp at the top of the picture that read 1:38 a.m. Me, the same girl who, four months ago, said she was too tired to talk at 9 p.m. because of rehearsals.

A month later, as soon as I touched down in LA, my only goal was to find an apartment. Unable to share the bedroom with my ex for obvious reasons, I shared the living room space with another roommate. His stuff fit in perfectly with the living room décor while mine was a thrown-together mess spilling into the dining area. It was, quite literally, the elephant in the room people walked around and avoided.

Every night, I slept on a twenty-dollar air mattress that would magically transform into a sheet by morning because all the air had seeped out. To make matters worse, my ex-boyfriend had the opportunity to vent about me left and right while I was gone, leaving all my roommates unsure about my character.

So you see, dear reader, I needed to move out. I desperately needed to find an apartment. With each apartment I visited, I daydreamed about all the ways I could be free from the current madness in my life.

The daydreams were so powerful, though, that they made me nervous. Every time I turned in an application, I was terrified they wouldn't accept it. Every time they denied me or granted an apartment to the person ahead of me, I was scared of being stuck in my living situation forever.

I was extremely thankful to Sheopatra for driving me to view apartments and drop off applications, but this inevitably granted her a front-row seat to my snowballing stress.

———

Tears threatened my eyes. With every fiber in me, I tried to keep my composure. Instead of focusing on the four phone calls that had gone straight to voicemail, I focused on the road ahead of me. Sheopatra did her best to console me, but it wasn't really doing much.

I'd been approved for an apartment last week, but I still hadn't received the keys. The landlord had rescheduled our meeting twice. Something about him going out of the country for a family emergency. Since I couldn't purchase the big items yet, I decided to get the little things: kitchen utensils, a toilet paper holder, a shower caddy, and other miscellaneous items. That way, I'd be ready for the bed, the couches, and the refrigerator as soon as those keys graced my fingers.

I glanced back down at the phone in my lap. Nothing. The

last time I'd spoken with the landlord, he said we'd finally meet today so I could receive my keys. But I was riding around LA with no meeting time, aimlessly purchasing home items. Four phone calls straight to voicemail later, I feared he would push the meeting back yet again.

Suddenly my phone buzzed. The long international phone number I'd become so accustomed to seeing came on the screen. A full ring had barely escaped before I picked up the phone.

"Hello?" I said as I signaled SHE to pull over. I wanted to take the call outside.

My landlord's accent was like music to my ears and my anxiety. "Eh, hello? Yes, Ms. Yorelis? I am sorry to inform you that you won't receive your keys for another week. Something came up and I must remain out of town for a bit longer."

In an instant, the music transformed into nails on a chalkboard.

"I'm sorry, what? Sir, I've already waited a full week for keys to an apartment listed as move-in ready. I understand things come up, but surely I can be accommodated in some way. Is it a possibility for you to ship the keys?"

"Yes, my apologies, Ms. Yorelis. That is a possibility. I must warn you, though, it is expensive to ship out of the country I am in."

"Nigeria?" I said, remembering our first conversation about his background. "How much is it going to be?"

"To ship these keys, it would be about three hundred dollars."

"Three hundred?! Sir, that's out of line. Because you caused this inconvenience, you should be the one to pay the shipping fee. This is outrageous!"

It was as if my decaying wallet had jumped out of my pocket and into my mouth, spewing nothing but the truth at my increasingly aggravating landlord. My mind went blank; my wallet and frustration continued the conversation for me.

"Sir, this entire process has been completely unprofessional. I was supposed to move in last week. I've already sent the security deposit and first month's rent. Three hundred dollars for keys I'm owed doesn't make any fucking sense!"

Before I could continue, my mind flashed through the events that had taken place in the past week and a half: Finding the listing online. Filling out an application that was only a page long. Sending the eight-hundred-dollar security deposit and eight-hundred-dollar first month's rent via Western Union because my landlord had already gone out of town, so I wasn't able to drop off a money order in person.

I remembered feeling so ecstatic, so overjoyed, that I was able to find a one-bedroom apartment in North Hollywood for eight hundred dollars, a unicorn compared to the steep prices of other apartments in the area. All that excitement was soon to be tested by my landlord's incompetence, his request for more money, and another trip to Western Union, 'cause this man—

Then it hit me. All my thoughts crashed down like glass slamming into concrete.

This man had scammed me.

12

life after scam

Now, as a somewhat seasoned Los Angeleno, I can pinpoint all the red flags I missed. First and foremost, an eight-hundred-dollar, one-bedroom apartment in any part of LA is unheard of. Back then, one-bedrooms in a decent neighborhood started at fourteen hundred dollars. Nowadays it's hard to find anything lower than eighteen hundred. Additionally, sending money via Western Union for any business transaction screams scam. And after renting three apartments and purchasing a townhome, I know it's a joke to wait over a week to receive the keys.

With the tour and what I was able to make before leaving Florida, I had about ten thousand dollars saved up. I paid three thousand dollars to join SAG, a union that allows dancers to perform in television and streaming work. Oftentimes, SAG will allow you to do a certain number of jobs before making you join.

My wife was able to do quite a few jobs without a membership, but the day she was supposed to work on an awards show, she received that infamous call from SAG: "Join the union or you can't do the job." I never received that infamous call, but I figured I'd join while I had the money.

With seven thousand dollars left in my savings, I sent sixteen hundred dollars to a man in Nigeria in hopes of getting my first apartment and moving out of my ex's. Then, after some much-needed help from Sheopatra, I found a studio apartment twenty minutes away from North Hollywood—the city center for most commercial dancers—for $950 a month. It was a find, my oasis! But I'm not gonna lie to you, reader; the neighborhood was SKETCHY.

After being scammed and then paying the security deposit and first month's rent for my *real* apartment, I was left with thirty-five hundred dollars. I left the remaining money in my savings and added three thousand dollars to it over the next two months. Then I walked to the used-car lot two intersections away from my studio apartment and purchased a 2003 Nissan Altima for six thousand dollars.

Despite being scammed, I would rate my money management in those early months in LA a six out of ten. I didn't let my savings get to zero. The car purchase dropped my remaining funds to $500, but a car is practically crucial in LA.

Public transportation in this city is not for the weak. Though I only spent two months using the bus and subway systems, which are fun-sized compared to New York's, that's a part of my life I'll humbly never return to. I've seen domestic abuse at bus stops. I've had to distance myself from people suffering mental health episodes on buses. And my poor nose. My sensitive, spoiled nose has smelled all the urine, feces, and rotten food that hug fabric bus seats and the corners of train stations. (To this day, I don't understand why *any* public transportation system would use fabric seats instead of plastic.)

Hell, my skin was even darker during those two months. Buses run anywhere from thirty to forty-five minutes apart, so I spent many days waiting in the hot Southern California sun.

That life isn't for the weak. Or for a young woman without pepper spray.

13
furnishing on a budget

Karina sat across from me at daycare when I was nine years old, and we've been best friends ever since. Practically connected at the hip. She's that person I was with so often, we began to look alike. When I started dance lessons at a studio in the area, I begged Karina's mom to enroll her as well. Years later, when I attended a magnet performing arts high school, I begged Karina to audition. That bond lasted throughout our college years, and then it came time to beg once again.

"You've been unhappy all this time, Karina. You're almost done with your program at Concorde. There are multiple Concorde schools in LA, so you can finish there, or finish here and then move there. No matter how much you try not to, you love dance. You should move. Try it out so you don't have to wonder what could've happened. At least you'll have a degree to fall back on. If it doesn't work out for me, I'll have to come home and pick up dance teaching jobs until I figure out my next plan. You have a plan B."

I wondered how I could possibly be capable of giving Karina such a talk. It took me months to muster up enough courage to move. Months of planning and working so that I could be as prepared as possible. How I ended up trying to convince Karina to move in less than a year is beyond me, but I did.

We had so many talks. I gave so many "How are you gonna know if you don't try?" speeches. Though I was unsure about my own journey, I was a thousand percent confident in Karina's. Ever since we were kids, talent was no issue for her. Her flexibility and body type meshed perfectly with the technical styles of dance. And when we transitioned into freestyle training, her creative brain took over, guiding her steps, opening her mind, and expanding her movement at the speed of light, almost as if she wasn't a beginner at all. I was in awe of her, so no other choice made sense. She *had* to move to LA with me.

Finally, Karina agreed. Then it was go time. We took on extra teaching and choreography jobs at local dance studios, saved money, and put our money together to ship her car across the country.

When I came back from tour, my only goal was to move out of my ex's and get a place Karina and I could call our own. A month later, after tons of searching, falling prey to a scam, and a sea of tears, we found a place: a studio apartment in North Hills for $950.

As soon as we signed the lease, we drove to the nearest dollar store and tore through it like a Black Friday sale.

Kitchen utensils, hangers, mugs, plates, cups, decorative hand towels—we bought everything we'd need for our new humble abode. To all my first-time apartment renters on a budget out there, don't sleep on dollar stores or ninety-nine-cent stores! I still have a knife I bought during the shopping spree for my first apartment. Compared to the higher-quality knives I've been able to purchase over the years, I still prefer my dollar-store knife.

Our next stop was Kmart, a store I hadn't seen since elementary school but that still had open locations in Los Angeles. At Kmart, we found two futons that were a little larger than twin mattresses for eighty dollars each. To this day, I don't think I've slept on anything harder than that spring-filled futon mattress, but it got the job done.

The last big purchases for our home were drawers. We each purchased two large plastic drawers for twenty dollars apiece. Karina lucked out 'cause she'd stored a plastic drawer in her car before it shipped to California, so she had three drawer sets.

We furnished—and I use the word "furnished" lightly—our first home for under five hundred dollars, a dream for two aspiring dancers from Tampa without family support.

Karina's family didn't agree with her choice to move to California, so they offered nothing but long telephone conversations about all the reasons she should move back home. My mom would've given me her last to help, but I refused to ask. On top of having two young children to support, my mom survived off of her disability checks. She was in no position to pay for her daughter's overpriced rent or furniture in California while keeping things afloat at home. She did offer sound advice, though.

"You know those bells, like the one we have on our porch at home?" Mama asked on the phone the day after Karina and I had settled into our apartment.

"The ones that chime in the wind? Yeah, what about them?"

"Buy some and put them on the back of your front door. That way you can hear whenever it opens. Your own alarm system."

To this day, every time I see or hear porch bells, I'm reminded of my mother, protecting me from across the country.

14
my sketchy oasis

Our studio apartment was a dream come true—750 square feet of space all to ourselves. It was in an older building with about thirty units. The majority of the tenants were long-term residents who'd lived there for over fifteen years. Unless they were still living with their parents, no other young adults were in the building.

Because there were so many long-term tenants, my apartment was one of the few renovated units. Granite countertops lined the kitchen. Beautiful light-gray, freshly laid laminate tiles lit up the floors. To my young brain, the closet with built-in, full-length mirrored doors was the epitome of fancy living. The apartment didn't come with a fridge or central AC; I later learned that many apartments under two thousand dollars don't. I was able to purchase a used fridge off of Craigslist for $160, and an air conditioning unit sat in the window.

While my studio apartment felt like fancy living, everything outside the complex's doors suggested the very opposite. Cars weren't required to move for street cleaning or anything, so piles of trash collected on the curb, and abandoned cars decorated the street. Police sirens and helicopters were part of the neighborhood's soundtrack most days. I thought I'd seen police activity back in Tampa, but nothing could've prepared me for high-beam helicopter lights shining into my window in the middle of the night while police looked for a suspect in the area.

The motels to the front and side of my apartment building never stood out to me. *They're just cheaper hotels*, I thought. *There's a lot more in this area compared to my ex's place, but what difference does it make?* I quickly learned that a lot of different types of people inhabited those motels. Some were rowdy, some were hard-working immigrants trying to find their footing, and many were prostitutes.

Before I continue, I'd like to say I have nothing at all against sex workers. Hell, sometimes I wish that line of work was legal in the States. Maybe it would be safer for all parties involved. Maybe prostitutes of all kinds would have safe spaces where they could make money without going to a sketchy motel in a sketchy neighborhood. I have no issues with it, but when a random man tried to purchase services from Karina while she waited for the bus, I knew for a fact we couldn't renew our lease.

Though our building was gated, you could prop open the main door or slip into the parking garage while the doors slowly closed. That's probably what the girl who stole my clothes from the laundry room had done.

There was a small laundry room on the first floor of the building, right next to the parking garage. Because only two washers and two dryers served all thirty apartments, I'd have to wait hours to wash, so I usually stuffed my dirty clothes into a suitcase and rolled it to the laundromat down the street. But one night at around 2 a.m., I was packing for an 8 a.m. flight. I'd gotten off set too late and the laundromat was closed for the night, so I was left with no choice but to use the laundry room in my building.

About an hour later, I went back downstairs to retrieve my clothes from the dryer. When I walked in, a young woman and her boyfriend were staring back at me—two faces I'd never seen in my apartment building before. Seconds after we made eye contact, my gaze traveled to the blue-and-white windbreaker she was stuffing into her book bag. The rest of my clothes were halfway out of the dryer, spilling onto the floor, and peeking out of her book bag.

I was infuriated, sleep-deprived, and ready to call her all types of profanities, but then my internal safety alarm went off. I considered the possible outcomes in this room with this girl and her boyfriend at 2 a.m. She was smaller than me, so I could definitely fight her off if I had to, but there was no way I could take her and her boyfriend.

The only thing that left my mouth was, "What are you doing?" Slow, slightly shaky, but firm.

The arm that was stuffing my windbreaker into her book bag slowly relaxed as she acknowledged my presence.

"Oh... Are these your clothes?"

"Yes, these are my clothes. Could you give them back?"

"Uh, yes," she stammered. "I'm sorry."

"It's okay, just give them to me."

Trying to keep calm yet sweating profusely, I put the clothes in my laundry basket as she emptied them from her bag. By the time I was upstairs in the safety of my apartment, recalling the story to Karina, the overwhelming feeling of fight-or-flight left my body and something else set in.

"I should've let her keep a shirt or a jacket or something," I said. "She apologized and returned the clothes as soon as I caught her. She must've really needed them. I could've given her some, but I was so scared. That didn't cross my mind until now."

Besides the sex workers and almost getting my clothes stolen, I loved my studio apartment in North Hills. It was the beginning of my story. Where my dream of living in LA came to fruition while I prayed for more.

My apartment manager was great. He was a young Mexican man in his early thirties who was helpful and always struck up polite conversation with me. His mother, on the other hand, was a different breed altogether. She was a delicate older woman no taller than five-foot-three. The way my apartment sat around the corner gave her the perfect view of my front door from her living room window. We were about a yard apart, but that distance too often felt like three inches. She was polite, speaking to Karina and me in passing as we entered and exited our home.

One time, she told us she'd been watching our front door for any suspicious activity since she knew we were out of town. I didn't bother to ask *how* she knew we'd been gone, 'cause she probably watched us roll out our suitcases from the comfort of her living room window. If she didn't watch us, she definitely heard us; over the entire year we stayed there, I only saw her living room window closed once.

To this day, I still don't know that woman's name. I referred to her as Señora, a product of my Latino upbringing, in her presence. But in the confines of our home, Karina and I called her El Hawkon, The Hawk. She had good intentions (I think) but observed our apartment like a hawk searching for its prey.

Part of me wondered if she was just a nosy older woman. During our short conversations, she always had news to report about our neighbors. Whether it was the latest person to move out or the couple that had an argument last night, El Hawkon knew. In this way, she reminded me of my grandmother.

Another part of me wondered if she felt the need to control the two youngest adults in the complex—two young women who worked odd jobs, didn't follow a nine-to-five schedule, and loved music and dancing. She didn't hesitate in the slightest before calling noise complaints on us for playing music at 2 p.m. And one time she swore that marijuana smoke was coming from our apartment when we were burning incense.

One late night after a performance, Sheopatra, our friend India, and I got into a car accident. The police were in the middle of a high-speed pursuit when the car eluding them turned onto a street and rear-ended us at fifty miles per hour. The impact forced us into a curb, crunching the car like a retracting accordion. Before this night, I'd only ever tapped a pole at a gas station and hit a few curbs while turning; I'd never experienced an actual, life-threatening accident. It was a very long night. We went to the hospital, waited hours for X-rays, and went home at around 3 a.m.

I don't know if it was the shock leaving my body, the throbbing pain in my back, or watching SHE clutch her right shoulder all night, but as soon as we got home, a wave of gratitude hit me. I dropped my bags, did a 180-degree turn, walked right back through the front door, and held on to the railing outside of my apartment. I dropped my head and repeatedly thanked God for our survival. With my head down and to the sky, with my eyes closed and open, while standing and dropping to my knees, I thanked God. After a few minutes, I walked back into the apartment and passed SHE, who planned to talk to God outside too.

I gave her about ten minutes before going outside to check on her. She was slumped over the railing with her head in her hands. When I began softly rubbing her back, her face emerged from her hands and I saw water in her eyes.

"I could've lost you and India tonight," she said.

"It's okay. We're here. By the grace of God."

"By the grace of God."

I went back into the apartment to grab a tissue. After SHE dabbed her eyes, she said she was going to take a quick shower.

"Okay, I'll meet you in there soon. I'm gonna stay out here for a few more minutes." I had to thank God one more time.

I placed my elbows on the railing and cradled my head in my hands. I heard SHE's footsteps moving away from me, followed by the sound of the apartment door being shut. Seconds after, I heard another door open.

"Con permiso, can you please stop walking in and out? I keep hearing the door slam and slam. I can't sleep."

Dressed in a long nightgown and house slippers, El Hawkon was staring back at me.

I quickly wiped away stray tears. "Um, yeah. Okay. I'm actually going to sleep now."

That's all I could say. I was distracted from my prayer, caught off guard, and in disbelief. We were in no way, shape, or form slamming our door. Maybe it sounded louder to her because she never closed her living room window and always fell asleep there in front of the TV. A visual I passed by most evenings when I got home.

El Hawkon was sweet. Her intense surveillance reassured me that no one would break in or steal a package without being detected, but it also pestered me at times. After one too many complaints, I was ready to leave her behind. She could play neighborhood watch with the next unlucky tenants.

15

music videos

This might be a little morbid, but when I found out Santa Claus didn't exist, Christmas was never the same. After extracting my hidden Barbie video camera from the tree and playing back the footage of my parents struggling to put the presents out quietly, the magic went away. Not all of it, but enough to make the holiday feel different.

Now, don't get me wrong; I still love Christmas. The movies, the family time, the uncanny way most humans become abnormally nicer. I adore the holidays, but if I'm being honest, a little magic was lost the day I found out Santa Claus didn't exist.

That's how I felt after being on set the first couple of times too. Set can be anywhere production decides to film: a warehouse at Warner Bros., a lot with the entire shell of a house built inside, or a park an hour away from LA on top of a mountain, like where my wife filmed an AT&T commercial years ago. The locations may vary, but a lot of sets feel the same. There will be cameras, talent holding areas, and—my favorite—craft services.

At first, being on set was exhilarating. It was and still is a firm reminder that I achieved my goals and will continue to do so. But even though I was grateful to be on set, it caused the magic of the industry to fade a little.

I loved watching music videos as a kid. Videos from artists like Missy Elliott, Usher, and Aaliyah exposed me to the world of dance outside of it just being a hobby. I couldn't believe these people on my TV screen were being paid to dance instead of paying for lessons at a local dance studio like I was. The costumes, the makeup, the iconic music—everything was pure magic.

Until I made it to my first music video set.

The 6 a.m. call time on a cold spring morning was a push, but coffee instantly rectified that. Instead of a sleek cat eye, the makeup artist's eyeliner trailed my eye like a Richter scale graph. No problem. Thankful to have brought my own supplies, I locked myself in the restroom and revived my face. For some reason the hairstylist had brushed out my curls only to rewet them with spritz, but I salvaged that too.

By the time the clock struck noon, none of the dancers had shot a single scene, even though we'd been camera-ready since 10 a.m. I maintained patience, turning my attention to the romance novel I'd brought from home. The story distracted me from the cold temperatures in the dancer holding area, a space in the parking lot that consisted of a tent and some chairs, without even a heater to ease our cold muscles. Despite all the trials working against us, I kept my composure. But when I saw the artist pull into the parking lot at 1:30 p.m. with a messy bun and no makeup, the blood drained from my face.

The fibers holding me together snapped in unison, and the reality of the day set in. We'd be lucky if we started shooting at 4 p.m., and that's only if the artist didn't take her time in hair, makeup, and wardrobe.

At 6 p.m. we finally started shooting the first scene, but the sun had set and cold air breezed through our already too-thin attire. The director yelled "Cut!" and "Action!" as if we had on-and-off switches implanted into our foreheads. Without any regard for our fatigue or the growing aches in our bodies, he continued to shoot the scene until we wrapped at one in the morning. And in the end, a dance section that took hours to film amounted to nothing more than seconds of exposure in a three-minute-long YouTube video.

That's an extreme example of a terrible music video set experience. Not all of them are that bad, but most will deliver their own kinds of discomfort: catering that doesn't meet your dietary restrictions, a circle of chairs instead of an appropriate holding area for talent, cold conditions, scorching conditions. The list goes on.

If I'm being honest, I believe *no* shoot is perfect. That's why, my dear reader, it's so important for you to find things that keep you grounded on set, centered and shielded from the inconveniences of the day.

Sitting around waiting? Unfortunately, it's common for music videos to shoot for anywhere from eight to fifteen hours.

You'll hurry to set, rush to makeup, and get dressed in seconds only to wait hours to shoot. Bring some things to help pass the time, such as your cell phone with a portable charger, a laptop, a book, or a card game. And when in doubt, talk it out. I've had some of my best times on music video sets just speaking to other dancers. I love getting to know people more deeply!

Sitting around in hard metal folding chairs? Buy an outdoor folding chair (I've gotten one for as low as ten dollars at Big Lots) and put it in the trunk of your car. You never know when it might come in handy outside of dance too. I've whipped out my trusty chair while waiting in the DMV line!

Picky snacker? Pack your own snacks. Food will make or break my day, so I always make sure I have backup options just in case catering is trash.

For one shoot, I sat in full makeup and wardrobe from 10 a.m. to 5 p.m. My costume was two sizes too small and the makeup didn't match my complexion, but I couldn't care less. Not only did the set provide individual trailers for each dancer, but they also rented a taco truck for the entire day. That trailer was my office. I caught up on emails, hit two thousand words in my manuscript, and watched a few episodes of a Netflix series, ordering a couple of tacos in between each task. It was fantastic! By the end of the day, I'd tried everything on the menu. When it finally came time to dance, my bloated tummy was seeping over my small outfit, but that didn't get me down. By then, I'd had one of my most peaceful days on set.

Bring makeup. You're a novice? That's okay. It's still vital that you have your own supplies—matching foundation, bronzer, mascara, lashes, and lipstick at the very least. If you get stuck with a makeup artist who applies blush like it's 1982 or changes the shade of your skin, you'll have a better chance of salvaging it if you have your own supplies. I'm even willing to bet that there will be a dancer who's nice enough to help you.

And here's my last yet most important tip: You have to *accept it all*. Don't watch the clock or count the time passing unless it's to document your lunch break. Accept that you won't be going anywhere for some time. Dwelling on it only makes it more unbearable. This goes for any time-consuming activity that doesn't care about your schedule, like waiting in line at the grocery store. No matter how much you breathe on the shopper's neck in front of you, or how many times you sigh loudly, the line will move at its own pace. Of course, this is easier said than done, but I promise that the more you implement this into your life, the less daunting tasks will become. Like sitting in costume and makeup for hours.

16
auditions

On paper, auditions look simple. You come in, learn a combination, and perform it for the artist or choreographer. But the hard truth is, they're usually way more complex than that.

The day begins when I get that fateful email: "Audition for Fulana's awards show." Most of the time, they send out the notices at least a day before the audition, but there have been a couple of times when I received an email just hours before. Either way, my mind goes into overdrive: Do I have a headshot and resume printed out? Do I have time to go get one? The email said "contemporary dancers needed," but I haven't trained in that style in years; will my skills support me through this audition? Do I have any clean audition clothes?

During my first couple of years in LA, I attended every audition I was honored enough to know about. It didn't matter if the dates conflicted with something else or if the choreographer wasn't a good fit for me; I was there, warmed up, with my head-shot in hand. Nowadays, I take more time to think before accepting an audition by asking myself a few questions: Does this job align with my morals? Is the rate acceptable? Is it worth it?

I've done too many jobs where I was uncomfortable with the artist, wardrobe, or dance steps. When another job like this comes along, I consider how much discomfort I want to allow into my life. I grant some jobs a certain amount of leniency. But when it comes to rates, I have become unwavering. My body is my instrument, and it must be fairly compensated for what it goes through.

And lastly, is it worth it? What do I get out of it—working with a new artist, good choreography, quality footage, developing a relationship with a new choreographer, nurturing a connection with a choreographer I already know?

Once I decide to go, the game plan begins:

1.   print out a headshot.

I've been a customer at Noho Copy & Print since I moved here. They're affordable and quick and will gladly ensure that your headshot meets industry standards, including proper picture paper, eight-by-ten measurements, and your name listed in the bottom corner.

Noho Copy & Print is one of my go-to places, but that's the case for lots of other artists in the Valley as well. Give yourself ample time to get that headshot and resume printed, 'cause you never know when you'll arrive to a line pouring out of the establishment. Also look up their hours before arriving. One time I parked in front of the printing shop with forty-five minutes to spare before an audition. After a quick scan of the desolate parking lot, I realized they were closed. I ended up at an audition for a major artist with two minutes to spare, holding a four-by-six, nameless headshot printed on regular copy paper. Thankfully the choreographer was my friend, so she just glanced at my terrible printing job, laughed, and moved on.

My dear reader, if you'd like to avoid this stress altogether, print a couple of copies out to have on standby before your next audition.

2. pick an outfit.

Even if it isn't noted in the email, there's an unspoken rule that you need to wear all black attire to an audition. Some people ignore this rule, and that's fine. I'm a fan of individuality! However, out of sheer laziness, I still wear all black. Black is easy to spot among my colorful clothes and is generally free of visible sweat stains. And because the color isn't a part of my everyday wardrobe, my black garbs are always clean and ready to go.

Some dancers whip out sexy black mesh unitards with tiny undergarments underneath. Others just make sure their clothes are clean, comfortable, not too homey, and relatively black (instead of the faded color that results from over-washing). I typically rock Yoe's Ol' Reliable: a formfitting top, baggy pants (lint-rolled to hide any evidence left behind by my cats), and Air Force Ones.

There's also a broad spectrum of acceptable hair and makeup styles. I'm the biggest advocate for doing whatever makes you feel your best. If that's curling your hair and beating your face to perfection, then by all means, go for it. My method, on the other hand, includes tinted moisturizer, mascara, lip gloss, and a slicked-down low ponytail. No matter what you choose, there are a few essentials: a shower, deodorant, and ChapStick. And if you're the type of person that sweats a lot, consider packing an extra t-shirt.

3. plan ahead.

Allot enough time to get dressed, do your hair and makeup, eat, walk your dog, and complete whatever other tasks you might have. Never trust your GPS in Los Angeles. No matter what time the system says you'll arrive, give yourself at least thirty minutes for unexpected events on the road. Parking can also be a nightmare, so grant yourself enough time for that as well. There's nothing worse than arriving at an audition, an already stressful environment, with your body in an anxious fight-or-flight mode because you rushed to get there. You can't control everything, but do the things you can control in order to stay stress-free.

After the essential prepping, your next hurdle will be to do the audition itself. Learning choreography at an audition is always a gamble. You never know what you're gonna get. On a good day, there are fifty bodies present. The choreographer teaches at a perfect pace. The routine isn't filled with unrealistic, back-breaking movements, but it still gives you a chance to display your abilities. But on a bad day, you have to maneuver around 150 bodies to find an inch of space to learn and dance. The choreographer teaches the routine at the speed of light. And certain movements in the routine threaten the safety of your instrument—your body.

It's up to you to find a process that helps you remain grounded amid all the chaos the industry has to offer.

When I'm learning choreography, I like to rehearse it full-out as much as possible. Anxiety permeates my body in different ways. Sometimes I get jittery, and even a simple step to the right is shaky and unstable. My lungs may start to function irregularly, with my breaths becoming short gasps for air. Doing the choreography full-out helps me release all the jitters and allows me to learn how to breathe properly while performing the routine. That is my process.

However, doing the choreography full-out too many times can cause other dancers fatigue, which would be counterproductive for the audition. Some dancers mark the routine while learning and wait for the audition groups to perform full-out. You have to experiment to find the process that works for you.

When it comes to the routine itself, always be open to trying new movements, but also use caution and discernment. There's a difference between attempting a groove you've never done before and trying to perform an acrobatic trick for the first time because it's in the choreography. Getting injured is never worth it, but *especially* not at an audition.

So, you prepped thoroughly and gave it your all in the audition, but for some reason the stars weren't aligned that day and you got cut. What next?

The unfortunate truth is, getting cut and hearing no are part of this career path. You might hear no more often than yes, but all it takes is that one yes to change everything. Rejection will happen; acknowledge your feelings but don't stay there. So many factors go into an audition: looks, style, height, racial preference, and then there's talent. Artist 1 might be looking for black dancers because eighteen out of twenty-five on the job are non-black. Artist 2 wants his performance to be more inclusive, so he's only searching for plus-size dancers. Artist 3 is five-foot-ten, so she doesn't want dancers who are shorter than five-foot-eight. The requirements vary.

On the one hand, I dislike the labeling in this industry. Shouldn't hitting the steps with undeniable skill be enough? I have a friend who is hands down one of the best, sauciest hip-hop dancers of my generation. Yet he doesn't receive a lot of opportunities to dance for his dream artists because of his five-foot-three stature. It saddens me that his height, something he can't control, plays such a prominent role in his career. His talent should speak for itself.

There's another side to these physical requirements that's beautiful to witness. At one time, people weren't considered for jobs if they didn't fit the perfect mold. Disabled people could never be dancers. Tattoos were frowned upon. The queer community had two options: fall in line with society or fall behind. Age and pregnancy could end a woman's career.

I'm blessed to live in a time when all kinds of people are sought out. Some artists are only interested in hiring plus-size dancers. I begged my mom for braces in high school because I needed a smile that was "ready for the industry." Now it's common to read modeling castings that say "Looking for unique looks, freckles, gapped teeth, and tattoos." Back then, no one would've cared that Artist 1's dancers were predominately white; now people are making efforts (for the most part) to diversify—to make their shows, brands, and products speak to everyone instead of a specific group of people.

If you get cut because production wasn't seeking your look at the time, that's okay. You can't fix that. Focus on the things you can control. Dance is an ever-changing craft you can always nurture, tweak, and improve.

Getting cut happens. Unfortunately, it's the name of our game. Sometimes it happens at the very beginning; you'll walk back to your car while the engine is still warm. Other times you give it your all for hours and get cut in the very last round. No matter the situation, find a way to pull yourself out of a funk when you get cut. Go visit a friend. Take a nice long bath. If you're a personality on social media, utilize that full face of makeup and make some content!

———

Unfortunately, the "struggling artist" stereotype is alive and well in the dance community. We're all trying to chase our dreams and make ends meet in one of the most expensive states in America. That's not a secret. It isn't some piece of classified information choreographers don't know about; they're well aware of the nature of our industry. That being said, I've witnessed too many cringe-filled situations where choreographers single out a dancer because of their headshot—something that can cost hundreds of dollars.

"Girl, who is this?"

"This headshot looks ten years old!"

"You don't have brown hair anymore!"

"This picture looks like it was shot on a phone!"

I've heard all of that and more broadcasted to a room full of dancers. Quality, industry-approved headshots can range anywhere from three hundred to seven hundred dollars. Updating those pictures with every single change in one's appearance would become expensive very quickly.

From a choreographer's point of view, I can imagine how hard it would be to examine a stack of headshots at the end of a long audition and try to match dancers' sweaty faces with the done-up, photoshopped perfection of their headshots. It would be easier if that dancer with brown hair didn't have an outdated picture with blond hair. However, that doesn't give anyone the excuse to embarrass people.

To the choreographers reading this, don't single people out and publicly embarrass them about their headshots. If you have critiques or suggestions, pull the dancer aside and tell them privately. Doing anything more is nothing but a power trip.

To dancers, don't let a choreographer bully you about your headshot. Do what you can do within your means. Visit EverythingYoe.com for a list of affordable headshot photographers you can start with.

17
rehearsal tips

Sometimes you'll warm up for an awkwardly long amount of time 'cause the camp decided to have a creative meeting before rehearsal. So there you'll be, an hour and a half after your call time, doing your fourth lunge and seventh neck roll, anticipating the start of the day. Other times, the choreographer will throw steps out as soon as everyone arrives, playing mental dodgeball with your brain. One time I entered a rehearsal, put my things down, began stretching, and fifteen minutes later, the choreographer announced ten dancers were cut from the project. In this industry the possibilities are endless. Every day is a roll of the dice; you never know what you're gonna get.

Among all the chaos, it's easy to experience emotional and physical stress during the rehearsal process. Not all the time, but it's more common than you probably think. Here are some quick tips to make the rehearsal process as enjoyable as possible:

1.   be on time.

Give yourself ample time to find parking, spill your coffee, clean it up, and be on the dance floor with time left over to warm up. Los Angeles traffic is unpredictable. I try to arrive at rehearsal with twenty or thirty minutes to spare, even if that means waiting in my car for a couple of minutes to pass the time. No car? Chill at a nearby coffee shop. If something completely out of your control happens, like sleeping through your alarm or getting into an accident, the choreographer might be more understanding if you have a timely track record. Plus, rushing causes added stress. Save your stress meter for any unexpected rehearsal blunders!

2.   pack the essentials.

Get to know yourself. Figure out what you need and don't need. Extra snacks? Shirts? For instance, I hate sitting in damp clothes for extended periods of time, so I pack extra clothes. I drink plenty of water to maintain hydration. And low screen time is one of my daily goals, so I try to keep books in my bag.

Here are some of the supplements I love to use during grueling rehearsals:

- Magnesium at the end of the day to aid muscle recovery. You'll be less sore the next morning!
- Whole Foods Wellness Formula, my favorite immunity vitamins to ward off sickness. Eight hours

of physical activity for six days out of the week can take a toll on your body. Consume the immune-support supplements that work for you!

- Amino acids before rehearsal for muscle hydration.
- Green tea. I quit drinking coffee, but caffeine still has me in a choke hold.

And here are some things I pack in my rehearsal bag: extra clothes, water, deodorant, body spray, a foam roller for my muscles, a book, a portable phone charger, and my laptop, just in case there's some downtime to write.

3.   get some sleep.

It sounds cliché, but rest is necessary for your body and mind to recover. Going out for a night on the town might not be the best decision if you have a 9 a.m. rehearsal the next day. I'll be honest and say I'm guilty of breaking this rule, but I always regret it.

4.   stretch and cool down.

Before 2019, I didn't know who "warm-up" was. I'd never heard of that man. A quick neck roll, a wiggle, and some hops sufficed. Then I suffered a few back spasms and slipped a rib twice. Don't learn the hard way like me. Stretch. Warm up. Be so warm that you're sweating before rehearsal even starts. And at the end of the day, cool down. Stretch again to combat the buildup of lactic acid and promote muscle recovery. Your body will thank you.

5. be patient.

Things change all the time. Concepts get swapped out. Roles shift. And during those perfectly hectic jobs, details don't solidify until the day of the show. As long as the camp continues to treat you with respect, try to be as patient as possible with the ongoing changes.

There are many working departments for something as simple as an awards show performance. Music might change because the performance overlaps with a commercial break. The network could decide to change every costume with exposed midriffs to appeal to conservative viewers. Hell, I've been on an awards show where the network scrubbed the entire performance 'cause they decided a song about the artist's parents getting deported was too "liberal." Shit happens. Brace yourself to the best of your ability.

I might've frightened you, but rehearsals are often my favorite part of the job. During breaks, I get to speak to the dancers and choreographers and learn more about them. Nothing motivates me more than a group of people heavily breathing, studying their bodies, and trying to perfect the choreography to the best of their abilities.

When I get to rehearse with artists like THECouncil, Tacir

Roberson, Luz Frias, and Idaliz Cristian, I know I will be fed physically and spiritually. Though they're all different movers, those women push me in ways I never thought possible. Their infectious energy is like iron sharpening iron. Watching Tyrik Patterson's creative process is like observing a mad scientist at work. His mind's running a marathon while his body seeps magical visuals that cannot be confined to just "dance steps." No matter what madness occurs on the outside, he keeps his cool, never taking it out on the dancers. I can't wait to see how far his career takes him.

When choreographers give us the full rundown of the project at the beginning of rehearsal, my mind usually screams, *What the hell?!* They quote songs I've most likely never heard. They present digital sketches of the stage that look like nothing more than color-coded shapes. At this point, the overall concept of the project won't be entirely clear to me. I love when the details finally come together, when the stage is sitting in front of my eyes instead of existing as lines on paper, the camera angles bring our movements to life, and the magic sets in.

There is magic in the chaos of rehearsals. I promise. It can be hectic, but it will end in beauty.

18
changed forever

Content warning: The following chapter contains material about sexual assault that might trigger PTSD or cause mental/physical distress.

The thick air stuck to my skin as the twelve of us piled into the passenger van. My makeup, once precise and crafted, drooped down my face with the humidity. The Miami crowd had given Letti so much energy, she decided to add extra songs to the set on the spot. She added ballads and other hits, and even took the time to introduce the audience to all her dancers. With the extra songs and late start time, we didn't perform our final number until 11:30 p.m. We were spent.

The ride back to the hotel screamed with silence until one of the dancers asked, "We still going out?"

"Uh..."

"I don't know."

"I'm kind of tired."

"I'm exhausted," I added. "Letti killed me with those songs she added. As if the normal show wasn't hard enough. I'll fall asleep at the club if I go."

Spurts of laughter traveled through the van.

"I kinda wanna go to the beach," Isabella said.

The beach—at night?! Her statement sent me into a whirlwind. No one would *ever* catch this Florida girl in the water at night, hopelessly blind to any creatures swimming near me. No ma'am.

Before I could open my mouth to express my fears, the choreographer, Noah, said, "I'll go with you!"

Isabella's face lit up. "Aw, really?"

"Yeah, let me just drop these bags off in my room and we can go."

A weight formed in my stomach. Having only done one job with Letti before, I was still new. New to the camp, new to the dancers, to the veteran dancers, and to Noah. We hadn't crossed physical paths, but his reputation had made its way to me a few times. His flirtatious antics and love for female dancers are well known around the dance community. I knew; the industry knew. But did Isabella?

I peered toward the back of the van. Her dreamy eyes looked out the window as we barreled down Ocean Drive.

She's the type of person to ask what your zodiac sign is. Angel numbers stick out to her on a regular basis. She greets and hugs everyone in the room upon entry, but she also has the body of a *Sports Illustrated* model. She stops men in their tracks in real life and on social media. I'm sure they see her curves before her barely-legal baby face. Hell, maybe I would too if I hadn't met Isabella when she was thirteen, prior to the wonders of puberty.

Would someone like Noah mistake her nineteen-year-old sweetness for more than friendly? How old was Noah, for heaven's sake? Based on his career accolades and the artists he'd graced stages with, he had to be thirty-five or older. What were his intentions on the beach, at night, with this young girl? My thoughts snowballed. I couldn't take it anymore.

"I'll go with y'all!" I blurted out. "I haven't been to the beach in such a long time."

Tension unraveled from my shoulders.

"I'll go too!"

I turned around to spot Elijah smiling in the back of the van. Before Letti, I'd never worked with Elijah, never heard of him. But after the first day of rehearsal, I would never forget a talent like his.

In addition to hip-hop styles, he was proficient in ballet and modern, and often used those skills during freestyle moments in the show. He never just walked on stage and began the choreography. He glided across the floor, flew through the air, displayed outstanding skills, and yet still managed to make it to his spot in time for the choreography.

He and the other male dancers, each equipped with their own superpowers, inspired me to explore different parts of stage performance. I wanted to see how far I could push the limits in rehearsal, how full-out I could execute the choreography, how I could make it my own, and ultimately, if I could keep up in a sea of men.

Besides me studying him from afar, or the good-morning hug I gave everyone at the start of rehearsals, we'd never spoken. He kept to himself for the majority of the eight-hour day. On his lunch break, he was either dancing his ass off or on the phone. Why he decided to go to the beach seconds after my announcement, I'll never know, but it was an immediate red flag.

"All right, anyone else going?" I scanned the van, making eye contact with the dancers who weren't drifting in and out of sleep. "Nobody? Okay..."

Weird double date at the beach at night, I thought. *Just great. Whatever. As long as Isabella is safe, 'cause I don't know any of these men like that.*

And that's how I ended up sitting on the beach in shorts and a t-shirt, watching Noah, Isabella, and Elijah strip down to their underwear and go swimming in the dark waves. With my legs crossed at the ankles and my hands clasped like a schoolteacher, I observed the scene while periodically playing with the sand around me.

It wasn't so bad to discreetly protect someone at 1 a.m., having had little sleep, while on a beach. After a few minutes, I allowed the sound of the waves to calm me. I silently prayed for their safety and sat a little closer to the tide, allowing the residual waves to reach my toes.

From what I could see, Noah was giving a little energy to Isabella. They wrestled in the water, had handstand contests, and crashed against every wave that came their way. It was kind of cute. I made a mental note to talk to Isabella the following day. She seemed to enjoy the flirtatious air between her and Noah. If she truly liked it, I wanted to know so I didn't end up chaperoning their escapades in the future. Their age difference wasn't my cup of tea, but it would be none of my concern as long as they were two consenting adults.

As the romantic beach movie between those two unfolded, Elijah third-wheeled for a painful amount of time. I wondered how many of his playful jokes and antics would fly past the couple too focused on each other to notice. Eventually, he took the hints and began swimming around on his own. Until he turned his attention to me.

"Yoe! Why don't you come in the water? It feels great!" He trudged through about two feet of water before reaching the sand.

"I'm good right here. Thanks!"

"Whew," he said as he plopped down centimeters away from me, wearing nothing but his ocean-soaked boxer briefs. "It's such a beautiful night."

My body stiffened. As a woman who has dealt with many small advances from men—asking for my phone number, pretending to be friendly before unleashing their feelings on me, or catcalling—I've gotten good at spotting the signs. One of them is sitting too close to me when there's plenty of space around us. An empty beach at night has a million places to sit, so my inner alarm rang immediately.

"Yeah, it's nice out here. I miss the Florida weather."

"You know, Yoe, I feel like you don't really like girls."

In a millisecond, my neck retracted and my face scrunched.

What the hell?

Despite the utter disrespect I felt, I took a breath and prayed that God maintained my cool. I learned very early on in my career that it sucks to have animosity toward someone you're touring with. From rehearsals to partner dancing, it makes the whole experience painfully awkward. It's hard to trust someone to lift you or effortlessly transfer weight after you've called them out of their name. I'd made that mistake once and decided that I would think before speaking in the future.

The only word I could conjure up was "Huh?"

"What I meant was, you don't really feel gay to me."

My face contorted, then I exhaled. "I'm sure you feel a lot of ways. But I can assure you I love women. Not that I need to prove that to you." An out-of-place chuckle reverberated from my chest.

"Please, Yoe. I'm not trying to offend you. I'm just saying you're young. Don't knock it till you try it."

"I've tried it before and it's not for me. Not that that's any of your business." I rolled my eyes and turned my gaze toward the ocean in front of me, watching as Noah and Isabella swam with the waves thirty feet away.

"Well, maybe you should try again..."

I felt wet lips brush against my neck. The skin he'd touched disintegrated. My eyes ignited. In one motion my hands spread across his chest and shoved him. Though he was sitting, the force caused him to lose his balance in the sand.

"What the fuck are you doing?" I stood up and put distance between him and me.

Deep breaths slowly expanded and contracted my lungs as I struggled to hold back tears. My eyes focused on the rise and fall of the waves.

How dare he? What is his issue? Can't he take a damn hint?!

My emotions were in such a vortex, I hadn't heard Elijah until he showed up by my side again, standing behind my right shoulder, whispering in my ear, "I'm sorry, Yoe. I'm just trying to show you what I can do. I can change your—"

Suddenly I felt him graze something along my right thigh. I felt wet skin and his fingers. I looked and saw it: Elijah with his briefs rolled down and his genitals in his hand, brushing them along my thigh. My thigh shriveled just as my neck had minutes ago. This time, my hands sprawled over his face and chest when I pushed him. The momentum combined with the uneven sand forced him to fall on his rear end just as a wave met the shore and collided with his face.

This time I couldn't fight the tears uncontrollably streaming down my cheeks. I couldn't stop my feet from leading me away. I just kept walking, short gasps escaping my chest, wondering, *Why the hell did he do that? What did I do to make him think that was okay? Why me, again?*

My mind flashed back to a year ago when a tattoo artist was

working on an elaborate thigh piece for me. At some point his coworkers left for the night, leaving us alone in the shop. As he cleaned the residual ink from my thigh, dragging his fingers along my skin longer than needed, goosebumps rose on my arms.

I started digging through my purse. "How much do I owe you again?"

"Oh, it'll be $350," he said smoothly, unaware of my discomfort. "Hold on, you got a little ink here..."

In one movement he closed the space between us, cupped my chin, and lunged his lips forward. If I hadn't retracted backward, his lips would've made contact with mine.

"What the fuck?!"

I pushed him, and the middle of his back slammed into the tattoo bed. For a second I fantasized about grabbing the same needle he'd tattooed me with and jabbing it straight into his leg. But I said nothing else, threw the money on the table, and left the shop, praying he wouldn't follow me.

Looking back, I wish I hadn't given him my money. I wish I would've strutted out of that shop with a free tattoo and my middle finger in the air. But I couldn't do any more than what I did in that moment. Only after the shock leaves your body do you think of other possible reactions. That tattoo artist made an unforeseen advance toward me, something I swore I would never let happen again. Now, here I was, tears soaking my t-shirt, and—

Wait, who's coughing?

Gurgling noises followed the labored coughs. I turned back

to see Elijah lying belly down on the shore. One after the other, waves thrashed his body around as he struggled to stand up. Then out of nowhere, chunks of vomit flew from his mouth, half washing away and half wading in the water with him.

It was impossible to tell whether he'd been choking on saltwater, vomit, or both, but I couldn't bear the sight any longer. Fed up with my instinctual need to be a good person, I angrily marched back over to him and stopped about a yard away from where he lay tangled in the waves.

"You okay?" I asked through gritted teeth.

"Uh, ahem! Yes," he gasped.

Without another word, I walked away, leaving him to continue battling the waves in four inches of water.

My steps led me to where the sand met the concrete sidewalk and benches. There, I used the public shower to rinse the sand from my feet and then waited on a bench for everyone to return from the shore. Isabella and Noah looked like two specks swimming in the distance. From where I was sitting, I couldn't see Elijah at all, nor did I want to. He was probably still tangled in ocean water and vomit.

Had he been drinking? Was that why he got sick? I'd heard rumors about Elijah's drinking problem, how he'd show up to rehearsals incoherent and reeking of alcohol, but I assumed it was an issue from the past.

Our hotel was within walking distance of the beach, but not close enough for me to travel alone at 3 a.m. Due to discomfort and concerned threats from my wife, I don't walk by myself at night, especially when I'm out of town. So I remained seated on the bench until the group returned from the water twenty minutes later.

The next morning, our tired bodies collected in the hotel lobby. Our flight back to LA was set to depart at 9 a.m., leaving us with a 6:30 a.m. lobby call. I was in the lobby thirty minutes before our call time. What was left of my night had been filled with packing, anxiety about sleeping through my alarm, and a sea of tears. My skin still prickled where Elijah had made unwanted contact. My eyes remained swollen and puffy, but dark sunglasses and makeup covered the evidence.

One by one, dancers exited the elevator with sleep-ridden faces. I greeted them with a half-forced smile, though I was relieved to no longer be alone with my thoughts. But when those doors opened and a smiling Elijah stepped out, my face flatlined and I buried it into my phone. He greeted all the dancers with an individual "Good morning." My eyes were occupied, but I could feel his presence slithering its way through the space from dancer to dancer until he stood just feet away from me.

"Good morning, Yoe!" he said brightly.

Without lifting my eyes from the screen in front of me, I said, "Wassup."

And that began a string of interactions where Elijah attempted to speak to me. Comments on the style of my luggage, small talk in the TSA line, random conversation. And every time, I met him with short, one-word responses while I fought tears behind my sunglasses.

By the time we lined up to board the plane, he'd had enough. I'm not sure if the other dancers noticed, but Elijah sensed my obvious animosity toward him. When I rose to take my place in line, he appeared in front of me with a sad look in his eyes.

"Yoe, can I ask you something?"

"Wassup."

"Did I do anything to you? I feel like you've had weird energy with me all morning, but you're talking to everyone else."

"I'm sorry, what? What do you mean did you do anything? You tried my life at the beach last night!" My face contorted.

Elijah looked confused, thinning my patience more and more.

"What? Oh, no... I don't remember anything from last night. I drank a little too much."

I wrangled my volume into a deep whisper to avoid causing a scene in the corner of this airport gate. "Yeah, I figured that when you were throwing up all over yourself, being tossed around by one-foot waves. But that was after you kissed my neck and put yo' dick on my thigh, talkin' 'bout some 'You ain't really gay.' What the fuck is wrong with you?!"

Elijah sighed, putting his face in his hands. "Yoe, I'm so sorry. I had no idea that happened. I'm so sorry if I disrespected you."

"If?!"

"I'm sorry *for* disrespecting you. Uh, is there anything I can do to make it up to you?"

"Make it up to me?!" I was stunned. "Honestly, I'm just trying to get on this plane so I can get home to my fiancée, so can you please just get out of my face?"

"Damn, there's nothing I can do at all?"

I picked up my carry-on luggage and met the other dancers in line. I couldn't believe he'd asked how he could make it up to me like he'd only stepped on my foot. The thought of his memory lapse disturbed me to no end. I couldn't decide if I believed him or not, and I couldn't distract my mind from it.

By the time the wheels touched down, most of my thoughts about Elijah had evaporated. All I could think about was getting home and crawling into Sheopatra's arms. I'd called her the night before, after a few fits of crying and screaming into a pillow. Between sobs, I recalled the events to her, but then the strangest thing happened: I transformed the detail about Elijah's appendage brushing my thigh into "He was in his boxers and pushed his pelvis onto me." I couldn't get my mouth to tell her what he'd really done. I'm not sure if it was embarrassment, fear, shame, or some cocktail of the three, but I lied to my future wife.

I don't remember her responses verbatim, but they were something like "What the fuck?!", "Fuck that man!", and "Do you want to tell Noah?"

"I just want to get on the flight tomorrow and come home," I told her. "I don't have any other jobs booked with Letti, so I don't even know if they'll include me in future gigs."

But somewhere in the back of my mind, I was convinced they wouldn't hire me again if I told them about Elijah. He had more years in the camp, and I was the newbie. It would be a no-brainer to get rid of me and hire another girl for future work. Another part of my mind wondered if I could handle working with him on future Letti jobs. Rather than rack my brain about the endless outcomes, I decided to cross that bridge when I got to it. When the prickling on my neck and leg wore off and tears stopped welling at the mention of his name, then I'd reveal the whole story to SHE.

But that moment didn't come until much later.

Over the following months, Letti performed at an awards show and filmed two music videos. I wasn't asked to be a part of any of these jobs. Thankfully, other jobs rolled in—performances with other artists and a commercial.

By this time, my entire demeanor had shifted. In the past I'd greeted dancers with a hug and a kiss on the cheek, a very Latino trait that had followed me out of Florida. When walking onto these new jobs, I no longer greeted everyone so personally. A head nod would suffice. (I still hugged most of the women, especially if I knew them before the job.)

If the job was long term, like a month or longer, my walls would naturally come down. But I remained on alert for any signs—signs that I may have missed with Elijah, such as prolonged eye contact, unnecessary touching, or any indication that someone doesn't take lesbian relationships seriously, whether I'm married or not. These days, I don't even care if a man is in a relationship 'cause, sadly, that doesn't mean much to the average male dancer.

There are diamonds in the rough. Rare unicorns in a pasture of horses. Devoted boyfriends and husbands in committed relationships. But the unfortunate truth is, that's rare among male dancers. So when a man tells me about his girlfriend or wife, I don't let up. My walls stay upright and strong as I patiently wait and see. Will he continue to behave weeks from now, or after a couple of Hennessy-ridden after-show parties? Or will one of the female dancers pull me aside to show me his 3 a.m. texts asking to drink wine and chill?

What Elijah did to me altered me forever. In some ways, I'm thankful for it because I'm no longer blown away when a male dancer flirts with me without any regard for my wife. I'm thankful because Elijah removed the veil and allowed me to see a lot of men for what they are without proper self-work. In other ways, I'm saddened by the walls and trust issues his actions forced upon me. I'm disappointed in myself because I now think twice before looking after young female dancers. Look where it got me last time.

19
triggered

I t had been two months since I'd spoken to Elijah, and I'd never felt better. Not only did he cease all conversation, but he also barely looked me in the eye. The choreographers placed us on opposite sides of the stage for most of the show. It was like working with nine dancers and a shadow. He hardly even existed.

With aching muscles, the other female dancers and I trudged to our dressing room. We were weeks into the tour shows, and they were beginning to catch up with our bodies. One by one, each dancer pulled up a chair to her assigned mirror. Showtime was in about three hours, and we had to use the time to prep our hair and makeup.

"Girl, I hate dancing while I'm on my period. I almost didn't make it through act four last night," one of the dancers said as she plastered foundation on her cheeks.

The banter that occurs behind the safety of a female dressing-room door is unlike any other. It's more than normal to talk about everything and anything, from menstrual cycles to body counts to greatest fears. I thank God for the solace dressing rooms have provided me throughout my career.

"Oh, you're on yours? I started yesterday," another dancer added.

"Mine ended a couple of days ago." I flashed back to the added fatigue my menstrual cycle always bestowed upon me.

"If y'all are on it, that means mine is coming soo—"

Jeanette, the hairstylist for the tour, suddenly bulldozed through the door. "What the hell is wrong with him?!" Her puffy eyes leaked with tears. Redness spread from her eyes to her cheeks and nose, like she'd been crying for a while.

"What's wrong with who?!" all of us replied almost in sync. We immediately sprang into action, grabbing tissues and hugging her. I slowly rubbed the top of her back.

Between sobs, she yelled, "Elijah! He's a fucking creep."

My stomach turned. My legs felt weak like I was walking on a boat in choppy water. Before she continued, I already knew what she'd say.

"I hugged him when I said hello, like I do with everybody. And during our hug, this man squeezed both of my ass cheeks—picked them up and dropped them!"

Gasps, contorted faces, and a couple of "What the fuck?"s spread through the room. The parts of my body Elijah had touched without consent prickled with heat. Contractions twisted my stomach, and moisture soaked my armpits.

These feelings had emerged months ago when I partnered with him for a day, but they were nowhere near this strong. They hadn't felt this strong since that night on the beach in Florida about two years before.

All I can recall is my breath quickening and the increasing heat coming off the vanity mirrors. I'm sure the other dancers remember this day far better than me, so forgive my lapse in memory. With every tear that fell from Jeanette's eyes, my anxiety heightened. With every tear she attempted to wipe away before it was replaced by new tears, my rage intensified.

I probably said a few words here and there. I remember another dancer trying to console Jeanette, who couldn't stop crying. I remember Jeanette saying repeatedly, "Why me? I don't wanna say anything. I don't want to seem like I'm too much. Like I'm causing issues. I'm only twenty years old. This is too much!"

I remember feeling like I was on a roller coaster, even though my body sat dormant in front of the vanity. Blood rushed through my veins. Tears gushed from my eyes. Beats reverberated from my heart to my eardrums.

Then I remember standing in the middle of the boys' dressing room, with little recollection of when I had gotten up and left ours. Old-school hip-hop played from a speaker in the corner as the male dancers sprawled out, doing different pre-show rituals: stretching, watching Netflix, scrolling through their phones, and Facetiming girlfriends. I spent a few seconds taking everything in, my eyes stopping at each person.

Do I really wanna do this? I thought.

I have no issue with confrontation, especially when dealing with scum like Elijah. But I'm wary about confrontation in public, specifically around male onlookers. You see, society has a funny way of deeming a woman "problematic" when she causes a scene. She's dramatic, emotional, and probably on her period. Meanwhile, a man causing a scene is blowing off steam or getting shit done.

Somehow, my body traveled over to the speaker and shut it off. I didn't yell, but my voice traveled. The words came out in a direct, serious tone. "You got one more time, Elijah. You got one more muthafuckin' time."

Blank stares followed me as I stormed away. Two of the male dancers barely let the door close behind me before catching up.

"Aye, I don't know what happened or what he did, but let me know if I need to do something about it."

"Yeah, you need us to handle him for you?"

Relieved tears pooled in the corners of my eyes. "No, y'all. I'm good, thank you. Elijah is just a weirdo, been a weirdo, and I'm tired of that shit. But y'all don't need to do anything. I have a feeling he's not gonna be here much longer."

Turns out, that feeling was quite the premonition, 'cause when I returned to the female dressing room, Jeanette was gone.

"She went to go talk to Letti's mom," one of the dancers said.

Though we rarely saw Letti's mom, she and Jeanette had grown close over the weeks. She often called Jeanette to her hotel room to do her hair before the concerts.

"To her *mom*?" I said. At that moment, any residual tears

became as dry as the Sahara. Amid tense, uneasy energy, I looked at the girls and smiled. "Oh, this is his last show."

He was gone. There was no way Letti's mom could hear this news and not act immediately. This was it. I would no longer have to see his face in rehearsals, on stage, or around the hotels. It was over, and I was absolutely elated. Relieved at the future absence of this scum of a man. But before my mood could turn around completely, something snapped. Somewhere deep inside, where my self-control hung by a feeble thread, *I* snapped.

My thoughts transformed from ease to a crimson-shaded rage. *This is his last show,* I thought. *So if he's gonna receive payback for what he did to Jeanette, for what he did to me, I have to do it now.*

Calm and collected, I unpacked my eye shadows and makeup brushes and continued getting ready for the show. The other women started having small talk, and I chimed in from time to time. When a few more male dancers knocked on our door to check on me, I returned each inquiry with a smile.

"I'm fine," I said. But behind every smile I flashed, there were sinister thoughts. I fantasized about the ways I could lay my hands on Elijah before the night was over.

My hands trembled as I did my hair. Earlier, anxiety and a little PTSD had caused my trembles. But this time, pure anger— the feeling of wanting to ram Elijah's face into a curb— produced the shaking in my fingertips.

Thirty minutes before the show, as I warmed up on the side of the stage, I fantasized about the different places I could give Elijah what he deserved. The hotel? His dressing room? My daydreams halted in one place: on the stage during the show. He would never see it coming.

There were a couple of walking patterns where I passed him on my way to a new formation. It would take nothing to send a knee directly into his groin and hop back into the choreography without missing a beat. I fantasized about my fists making full contact with different parts of his face—my knuckles gracing his jaw, his cheek, the center of his nose. I wondered what it would feel like to strike him with the point of my elbow over and over again.

"Damn, Yoe! You not playin' with this warm-up!" a dancer said, interrupting my thoughts.

Without realizing it, I had done push-ups to an entire song, which was drastic compared to my usual limit of ten or fifteen. Now that my coworker had brought me back to earth, I felt a tingling sensation immediately travel up my arms—a painful reminder that I'm not the person who does push-ups or work-outs in general. I laughed it off and continued warming up for the show, my mind wandering in and out of violent thoughts.

From the first act to act three, I couldn't shake the feeling. With every formation change, I couldn't stop my eyes from wandering across the stage, wondering where Elijah's spot was. I couldn't focus on a single dance step; my body performed the choreography on autopilot. Muscle memory from weeks of shows and months of rehearsals guided my movement, while my mind created thousands of scenarios. One image brought a big smile to my face: Elijah at center stage in the fetal position, holding his crotch after it had made contact with the hardest part of my knee, in full view of the entire crowd.

I daydreamed about the pain in my knuckles after they'd repeatedly met his jaw. I didn't even care if he hit me back, as long as I got in some licks he'd never forget. Licks that would sit with him, just like his unwanted touch sat with me.

I wanted to do what I didn't do that night on the beach: beat his ass. That push wasn't enough for me. It wasn't what he deserved. Back then, I felt like I had too much on the line. Elijah was a vet in the camp and I was a newbie, and I didn't want my job to be at risk. I didn't want to be labeled as the problematic girl. I also feared being labeled a liar. Now, I didn't give a shit.

Residual anger lived in the corners of my body because I hadn't fully dealt with the situation. You see, I was in my early twenties when Elijah did what he did, just a couple of years out of high school, and I'd transitioned into an adult world where things couldn't be handled the way I was used to. I was accustomed to verbal and physical altercations with flying fists, lots of profanity, and not a single care about whether onlookers were nearby.

On my first tour at the age of nineteen, I quickly learned how different adulthood was. I couldn't cuss my coworker out after she'd said something sideways to me. Because she'd delivered her nasty comment in a normal voice with a smile, I was considered "too much" or "too aggressive" for my loud, profanity-filled response.

In high school I learned that if you cuss someone out, you have to see that person in the halls or in classes for the remainder of the year. You're forced to navigate that unsettled, often-awkward energy. On a tour bus, that energy is in your face every day because you're *living* with that person, so your living space becomes awkward and unsettled. Learning these lessons so early in my career forced me to alter my natural reactions. I couldn't cuss people out so easily or put my hands on people.

I was intensely focused on these new ideals. So with the added fear of losing my job, I did nothing that night on the beach with Elijah except push him to the ground. Just a shove that sent him stumbling into the sand, mostly due to his high alcohol intake.

I wanted to do what I didn't do that night on the beach. I wanted to beat his ass like I was a grown man. I craved revenge. I longed to punish him for an unwanted act committed against my body.

Despite the revenge-filled thoughts plaguing my mind, I managed to make it to act five, the last part of the show. I don't know what lifted my mood. Maybe it was the endorphins from dancing, the extra-vibrant crowd we had that night, or an inability to hold on to rage. But somehow, I ended the show with a smile on my face and little anger left.

While walking on stage for the final bow, my mental wheels turned:

Jeanette talked to Letti's mom.

That woman doesn't play.

This is definitely his last show.

This is the last time I'll have to see his face on stage or in a rehearsal.

This is a cause for celebration.

I need to celebrate.

As we collected in a tight circle at center stage and put our hands in like a sports team before a big game, I locked eyes with Elijah, who stood directly across from me. Before throwing our arms up to celebrate another show accomplished, I decided to celebrate a little victory of my own.

I inhaled, and then with every piece of tension and trauma in my body, I yelled, "Congratulations on your last show, Elijah! Ya fucked up this time!"

I yelled over the music just a few inches away from Letti's mic, which could've picked up my words. I yelled for Jeanette. I yelled for myself. I yelled for all the women in the dance industry who have an "Elijah story." I yelled in celebration of us all.

20
fired...again

Crumbs dropped all over my lap as the overwhelming smell of tuna enveloped my car, but I couldn't care less. I scarfed down the food, wondering why the hell production hadn't released us for lunch instead of mass-ordering salads for us. The minute they released us, I hightailed it to the closest sandwich shop. Surviving a nine-to-five rehearsal with nothing more than lettuce in my body was agony, but if I didn't get any carbs before my next rehearsal from 7 p.m. to 11 p.m., I would surely perish. As the last few bites disappeared into my mouth, I couldn't help but wonder how I thought it was a good idea to do two jobs at the same time.

I'm not talking about step-touching and lip-syncing in a fake choir for one job and cheering in the stands as an extra in the other. Both jobs were laborious. Demanding. Calling on all the skills I worked so hard for in my teens.

The first job, choreographed by Lady E, was a four-minute New Year's special—a marathon compared to the usual two-minute routines allowed by television. In this piece, we traveled across the colossal stage, hit strong jazz-funk lines, and struggled to look pleasant while our stamina fought through the trenches.

The second job, choreographed by Jeremy, demanded strong authentic hip-hop, for he hailed straight from New York, the birthplace of the style. The routine was a two-minute section of a music video that made us feel like we'd been shot out of a cannon the entire time. Limbs were flying. Hair flipped and flopped in all directions. And at the end of each run, we were gasping for air. But I would only know this on day four—the day I rehearsed for eight hours, scarfed down a sandwich, and began Job 2.

After inhaling the sandwich, my eyes shot to the clock on my car screen. Cool, it was 5:26 p.m. Rehearsal didn't start till 7 p.m., so I had just enough time to stop by the nearest Target, buy a shirt to replace my drenched one, and maybe even take a cat nap. After purchasing a new t-shirt, a pack of underwear, and pants, and changing in the store restroom, I rolled into the parking lot of my second rehearsal location with forty-five minutes to spare, ready to nap. I switched the car to park, set my phone alarm to 6:50 p.m., laid my chair back, and watched the back of my eyelids.

At around 6:30 p.m., the sound of my ringing phone jolted me from my dreams.

"Nini? Hey, what's up?" I asked.

"Hey, love. I'm doing this music video job with you, and I can hear Jeremy asking Kourtney where you are."

My eyes cut to the clock: 6:33 p.m.

"What? I thought rehearsal started at seven?"

"No, it started at six."

I pulled up the email from my agent. "Nini, my agent told me seven to eleven. I've been in the parking lot eating and napping! I'll be right there."

"I'm so sorry, girl. Just come in and tell them."

My hands moved rapidly, grabbing trash, putting on Chap-Stick, laying frizzy hair, and spraying perfume to mask the remnants of my previous rehearsal. When I jogged into the studio, the rest of the dancers were in the middle of the floor, several eight counts into the routine. Kourtney's eyes nervously met mine. Then she turned to Jeremy, who ignored my presence entirely.

I set my bags down and attempted to hop into the dance, wondering, *Why didn't Kourtney call me?* She'd texted me earlier that week asking if I was available for this job. She was the person I had more experience working with. Live performances, awards shows—Kourtney and I had weathered those storms together multiple times. Nini was my friend too, but she didn't have a hand in casting me for this job. Inquiring about my tardiness wasn't her responsibility; she was just being a good friend, which only multiplied my love for her. My heart fluttered at the thought of genuine people like Nini, but at the same time, I became wary of Kourtney. No matter how many times my brain circled the topic, I couldn't fathom a reason why she didn't call to check on me and now she couldn't look me in the eye.

Jeremy, probably annoyed with my tardiness, refused to go back to the beginning of the combination so I could catch up and instead continued teaching. I did my best to catch the new steps while putting together fragments of the first half. When the group moved, I moved after. When they stepped to the left, I clumsily followed a few seconds later. It was like a weird adult game of Simon Says. Once the choreography had finally begun settling into my muscle memory, I started adding more personality, bits and pieces of myself.

"Hey, uh, Yoe." Kourtney appeared behind me during a water break.

"Hey, girl. Sorry I was so late. My agent told me the rehearsal started at seven."

"No worries. I just wanted to let you know, I see you hitting the choreography, just make sure to add your own steez into it. You aren't from New York, but you got that Florida sauce. Add some of that in there."

"Um, all right. Cool. Got you."

I wasn't sure what else to say, though I could've said something like, "I've been playing catch-up for most of this rehearsal, so how am I gonna add 'sauce' to something I don't know? Oh, yeah, choreography aside, why didn't you check up on me when I was late instead of acting like a scared intern? We're too grown for this!"

Nevertheless, I wrapped up my swirling thoughts, put my water down, and continued to go over the steps.

After running the piece all the way through, my chest heaved up and down. A part of me still couldn't believe we'd learned the whole piece in a couple of hours. Jeremy stood by the stereo observing the room's heavy breathing. He scanned us as if he were going to keep tweaking the routine, put us in formations, or give us the rundown on the shoot in a couple of days. The room was silent except for our breaths, the atmosphere growing more awkward by the second.

Then Jeremy finally said something to Kourtney, who was sitting nearby. "Ugh, dancers from New York are just different. Right?"

"Truth!"

They laughed together as I searched for the joke. After taking a closer look at the room, I realized only three out of the fifteen women were from New York.

"All right, let's run it again."

He turned on the music. The intro of the song rang through the speakers, and the dancers readied themselves for another challenging run-through.

A few extra seconds passed before my body felt prepared. *Just different?* I thought. *Did he mean what I think he meant?*

When the music ended and our breathing served as the only audio, my internal question was answered. Jeremy stepped onto the floor to explain a jumping groove from the choreography. He demonstrated the move more slowly to highlight which muscles should be activated. "Make sure this groove rolls through your back before you hop. All the way through. Don't skip any steps."

A mix of nods and yes's popcorned through the studio.

"All right, let's run it again." As he walked back, Jeremy made a silly face toward Kourtney, who was stretching inches away from the stereo. Before starting the music, he looked at Kourtney again and said, "If this job was based in New York, it wouldn't be so hard to teach this. No one dances like us."

The introduction of the music drifted back to my ears, but nothing could drown out Jeremy's statement. While marking through the routine, I came up with a few comebacks of my own:

"If you only wanna work with NY people, then hire 'them!'"

"Don't do otherwise just to hate the entire time and shit on us in the process."

"Wonder why the artist didn't do the project there since it's so great!"

"You know what? Battle me 'cause you're not gonna act like we're the bottom of the barrel in here."

I know quite a few dancers from New York, all very sweet and talented. I have no animosity toward them or their city, but I was ready to battle Jeremy anyway. None of that mattered, though, 'cause things are handled a little differently in the choreography world. Nevertheless, I continued fine-tuning the choreography and catching up on the details I'd missed. As more time passed, my attitude cooled and I tried to see the good in Jeremy's statement. *Maybe he's just missing home,* I thought. *I miss the Florida dance community every day. What if he just misses his dance world, the type of energy and movement that are natural to him?*

"Hey, Yoe?" Kourtney appeared at my side as soon as the music cut off.

Jeremy stepped outside while the rest of the cast took a water break.

"What's up?"

"You're doing great. Just put more of yourself into it. That raw Florida essence, you know? Your vibes."

This second round of critique released a procession of red flags in my mind. I openly accept help and correction, but something about this situation didn't sit right with me.

"Kourtney, did you vouch for me to be here? I heard Jeremy doesn't like hiring dancers he doesn't know. Is that how I got here?"

"Yeah, I did. You're hard as hell, friend, and I didn't care if he knew you or not. Once he sees what you can do, it's a wrap."

"All right, friend. I'll do my best."

The cycle continued: Running the dance until our lungs pleaded for air. Strange looks from Kourtney, none from Jeremy. More critiques and uneasy energy permeating the air. By the end of the night, the weight of the day sat heavily on my shoulders. From an eight-hour rehearsal, to the shock of receiving the wrong call time for the next rehearsal, to playing catch-up, to working with a choreographer who openly wished for other dancers to be in the room... By the end of the night, everybody's weight had become too much to bear.

Seconds after turning on my car, Kourtney appeared at my window. "Hey. So it was good, but—"

"Sis, I did me in there," I said, interrupting her. "I came in late; that was out of my control. I caught up in the choreo. I put my own flavor into it, but not as much as I could because I rushed to catch up. The movement isn't in my body yet. Now, if they bring me back tomorrow, after some sleep and marinating, I will eat everyone in that room up. Promise. But if not, I understand."

Kourtney's response was nothing more than filler. Something along the lines of, "I understand. Love you and good night." But I had no energy for her. The only thing left for my body to perform was a shower and a fabulous crawl into bed.

Right before my eyes closed that night, my phone buzzed with an email from my agent.

Subject: Test/Rehearsal Tomorrow

Hello, everyone. Tomorrow's rehearsal will be from 3 p.m. to 10 p.m. There will be COVID rapid-testing in Burbank at 10 a.m. Please forward your test results to me.

I set an alarm for 8:30 a.m. and allowed my body to sink into the mattress.

———

"Oh! Hey, Yoe!" Kourtney said when I arrived at the testing table.

"Morning!"

Then Jeremy walked up, doing a double take at me as if he'd seen a ghost.

"Good morning," I said.

"Morning," he replied.

I greeted the rest of the dancers as they arrived, the testers swabbed my nose, and then I got back in my car, ready for the nap that would prepare me for rehearsal later. But as soon as I unlocked the front door to my home, my phone buzzed with another email from my agent.

Subject: Music Video Release

Hey Yoe,

Unfortunately, production has decided to release you. Jeremy and the team are going to use a smaller number of dancers for the project. You will be paid for the rehearsal you did attend, so could you fill out the paperwork attached?

Everything finally made sense—Kourtney's "Oh!", Jeremy's shocked double take. They'd meant to fire me from that job way before the COVID test. Perhaps my name had slipped through the cracks and somehow ended up on the rehearsal email. I wasn't sure, but I did know that Kourtney and Jeremy hadn't expected to see me that morning.

———

Being fired from the job had taken a weight off my shoulders. Free from the politics of working with a new camp, free from

Kourtney's side coaching, and free from hearing about how much better New York dancers are, I poured my energy into finishing the job with Lady E and then moved on to the next.

I accepted it. Things were peaceful—until the music video dropped a month later.

No matter how far I scrolled through social media, I couldn't escape it. The entire dance community was liking, posting, and talking about it. Critiques tore it down. Supporters amped it up. People even turned the music video into a challenge, saturating the internet with their interpretation of the choreography.

That music video haunted me. And every time it played, I was forced to see the same number of dancers from the one rehearsal I attended. They hadn't downsized; they'd just subtracted me from the equation.

The footage jabbed my ego each time it graced my phone. I'm not the best in the world by any means, but I am top-tier. I'm a master in my field, and I've worked my ass off to attain this skill level. I'm revered by many dancers in this community. Hell, I'm revered by most of the dancers in that music video. Ask other dancers in the community, ask ex-coworkers—ask them what it's like to dance beside me on stage, and they'll say it's nothing but energy and talent.

Crippling humility used to prevent me from uttering, much less thinking, such words. Once upon a time, I was scared to speak like this for fear of being seen as cocky. But if I've learned one thing in this industry, it's that you must demand respect for your craft. If you don't believe in yourself, who will? If you don't demand respect, people will take advantage of you.

After my ego recovered, I realized that no matter how good you are, you still might not be someone's cup of tea. Before this, I'd been fired from another job, but it didn't hurt at all then. In fact, I was relieved. That camp had been predominately white and riddled with triggers and microaggressions. I thanked God for plucking me from that situation at a time when I didn't have the strength to walk away myself. But being fired by Jeremy, a black artist working with a cast of all black dancers, hurt like hell.

This wound had scabbed up, only to tear a little every time the video showed up on my social media feed. A wound that left behind scar tissue after I thought it had healed. Skin that tingles a little whenever I see Jeremy's face on the internet. But after a lot of prayers, crying spells, and aggravated screams into my wife's patient ears, it got better. I grew. I came out on top. Because no matter what Jeremy felt during that moment, I trust in my God-given talents. I am a force in this industry, and I know for a fact he hasn't seen the last of me.

21
f my feet

Sadly, I've been fired or let go quite a few times in my career. I saw some of them coming. Other times, the news hit me like a ton of bricks. However, the following story is different. This time, I knew that I was getting fired.

Working with Frida is on most dancers' bucket lists. Her visuals and choreography are timeless, provocative, and award-winning. Her name carries weight in our community. After doing some spot-date shows with Frida, I felt like my resume went from gold to platinum. I was one step closer to becoming a powerhouse in the industry.

I was ready for the difficult choreography; all those classes and conventions had sharpened my skills to a fine point. But nothing could prepare me for the grueling work environment.

Our schedule was no different from most camps. Dancers rehearsed for the first half of the day, and then the artist joined us for the latter half to learn the routine. These two halves of the schedule had about as much in common as fire and ice. At the beginning of the day, everyone was cheery, enthusiastic, and productive. We perfected the choreography while joking around in between sessions. Oscar, the choreographer, granted us short breaks so we could hydrate and regain energy.

Then the storm arrived.

Oscar, who was usually charismatic and confident, shriveled to the size of a raisin. The energy from the veteran dancers—those on the camp for five or more years—shifted from bright and bubbly to morbid and dull. Assistants scurried around the room like chickens with their heads cut off, plugging in multiple peppermint-scented diffusers because Frida never rehearsed without them. We could quite literally smell her arrival.

Over the entire three weeks I worked for Frida, she never spoke to me once. She never spoke to *any* of the new dancers. Perhaps it was a coping mechanism for trust issues with new faces. It's not that artists should greet me every day; however, I do believe a bare-minimum level of respect needs to be shown toward the people bringing your show to life. A simple "Hey everyone!" would've sufficed, but she never showed us such courtesies.

Frida appeared in one of two ways: silently or loudly. Silently, she'd descend from any corner of the room like a sorceress and tiptoe toward us, often catching the tail end of us running the routine or having side conversations. Because the choreographer and the veteran dancers often ridiculed Frida behind her back, these silent arrivals gave me the most anxiety. But no matter how many times they verbally dragged her, Frida never caught them. Other days, her entrance was just as loud as the peppermint smell in the room. She'd parade in with a BTS crew, an instrument, or her children.

We never knew what was in store when Frida arrived. One time, she strolled into the middle of rehearsal with a ukulele in hand, completely disrupting our routine. Oscar awkwardly shut off the music as Frida broke out into a song while she played the instrument. A mix of admiration, confusion, and stifled laughs spread among us as we cheered her on. I was so tired that I welcomed any distraction with open arms, so I cheered for Frida like I was at a Lil Wayne concert. When she finished, I hollered, "More! More!", and she played three more songs for us.

Later that week her two children, who were five and seven years old, sprinted into the room minutes before her in the middle of rehearsal. They bulldozed through our formations, pretending to perform the steps with us. Since I adore children, I also welcomed this distraction with open arms. Frida spent most of the time in a meeting with Oscar while some of the dancers and I played tag, hide-and-seek, and freeze dance with the kids. But when two hours had passed and I was chasing a child who had stolen my phone, my patience dried up. I exchanged pleading looks with the nanny, but she just sat back in her chair like she was on vacation.

These moments were a complete waste of time, but they didn't bother me too much. I just let the time pass, waiting for

Frida to decide to work. When she wasn't making grand or spy-like entrances, she was very involved. While learning choreography, she paid attention to detail and worked hard to perfect it. She suggested lots of modifications, which Oscar accepted willingly—or at least his poker face did.

Frida's personality was like a live caricature. Every nuance was so dramatic and larger than life that even when she tested my patience, or didn't exhibit the manners I preferred, I didn't take her too seriously. She was something straight off a reality TV show; even if you hated it, you couldn't stop watching.

Things didn't reach a boiling point until about two weeks later.

First off, I couldn't for the life of me understand why we were rehearsing for a music video for three weeks. These jobs usually last three *days*, a week at most. In the beginning, my wallet didn't mind earning a rehearsal check for that long. Yes, please! But after week two, my fatigue screamed, *Why the hell would anyone rehearse for a music video for three weeks?!*

"Once everyone has their costume on, we'll do a lineup," Frida announced as she disapprovingly scanned the clothing racks.

I could see pools of sweat dampening the wardrobe team's clothes from across the room. I didn't blame them; Frida had walked in prepared to dislike the options, rolling her eyes and sighing at the collection of garments before they were even on our bodies.

"A lineup?" I whispered to a veteran dancer.

"Yeah, we all line up and she examines our outfits one by

one, telling the wardrobe team what she hates and likes... Well, mainly what she hates."

The blunt honesty made me chuckle. "Okay, but will I be wearing my own shoes or these wooden death traps?"

Frida's preferred dance shoe was a torture tool. They hurt her feet too badly to break them in, but instead of searching for a better shoe, she forced all the female dancers to wear these shoes during rehearsal. I still couldn't get my mind around how she'd miraculously hired five female dancers who wore a size eight-and-a-half.

Every day, one of us had to wear those dreadful shoes. They were as stiff as an ironing board, too narrow, and just plain ol' ugly. We were living our version of *The Sisterhood of the Traveling Pants*, only the pants were unbending torture devices that dug into the sides of our feet.

"Wooden death traps?" the veteran dancer said. "Hell yeah. She's gonna give us hell if we don't break them in for her."

"Ugh, these blisters are getting really bad. If she wants me to keep running this routine, Imma need a break," I said.

Her shrug was a warning: *Do you, girl. Good luck.*

Before heading to the dressing room, I pulled Oscar aside. "Hey, can I take a break from these shoes for the rest of the day? They're giving me really bad blisters."

"Uh... um..." His eyes darted from side to side as if Frida had detachable, floating ears that were listening in. "For the rest of the day? Uh, yeah, I guess. I'm not sure how Frida is gonna feel about that, but sure. Go ahead. Rest your feet. It's fine. It's totally fine."

His nervous rambling was hard to witness, but the only thing on my mind was freeing my aching feet. Seconds later, I yanked those witch shoes off, left them in the middle of the dance floor, and went to the dressing room.

"His pants are hideous," Frida said, interrupting my thoughts. "Get him another pair. And make sure they aren't scraping the floor like these. Hem them."

"Got it," the head of wardrobe said with a shaky voice. It sounded like nails on a chalkboard, like the word vomit Oscar had produced earlier. Everyone working for Frida was the same, always anxious and cowering.

Day by day, things chopped away at my patience: Long rehearsal days. The constant fear of Frida. Keeping up with her antics like I was sprinting across a tennis court. And the most annoying part was, I had to deal with all of this while breaking in her stupid, overpriced heels. I hadn't realized it then, but I was in a pressure cooker, slowly reaching my limit.

Frida had finally made her way to my end of the line. Her gaze inspected every corner of my costume. It was the most eye contact she'd given me on the entire job, though it technically wasn't for me, just the garments on my body.

"All right, let's shorten Yoe's skirt and make her top a halter instead."

Prior to this moment, I didn't know she knew my name, and she'd said it this time only to critique my outfit. How can someone stare at you and say your name, but somehow still make you feel like nothing more than a piece of dust in the room?

"Yes, ma'am." The head of wardrobe scribbled down her notes at the speed of light.

"Also, these black fishnets need to go. Put her in flesh-toned ones instead."

"Got it."

Before moving on to the next dancer, she paused, scanning me up and down.

"I heard you don't want to wear my shoes."

I hesitated, completely thrown off that she'd acknowledged my presence. My eyes cut toward Oscar, who was standing a couple of feet behind her, and his face drained of all color. He was obviously responsible for providing Frida with this fun fact.

I snapped back to reality and replied, "Yes, I'm taking a break. They're hurting my feet and giving me blisters."

She curved her lips into a small, condescending smirk. "Oh, you'll be fine. Everyone takes turns breaking in my shoes here. Blisters are a rite of passage."

I wondered how my face looked, 'cause it felt like my left eye was twitching like a malfunctioning robot. My mind raced, and the words left my body before I could stop them.

"Oh! So fuck my feet, right?"

The pressure cooker whistled. The other dancers immediately stiffened. Oscar's expression froze like Medusa had turned him to stone. I blinked multiple times, surprised by my own words—free of filters, restraint, and tact. Frida's eyes flickered blankly. I couldn't read her expression. It was stoic. Stiff. Almost glazed over, as if she were sleeping with her eyes open. After a couple of seconds that felt like an eternity, she tightened her lips into a hard line and continued to the next dancer.

When I got home later that night, I showered, popped open a bottle of wine, and binged a Netflix series without any care for my bedtime. Why worry about going to sleep early? There was no way they'd call me back to rehearsal after that outburst. "Fuck my feet"? Who curses at the artist and returns to rehearsal the next day?!

By 9:45 p.m., the crystal-clear answer to that question arrived in the form of an email:

Rehearsal at 10 a.m. tomorrow.

They must've sent it by mistake. Maybe no one had updated the tour manager on my recent unemployment. Surely some-body—my agent or Oscar—would call me to break the news: "Sorry, Yoe, but this is the end of the road." I refreshed the email app every couple of minutes, but nothing came. By 11:00 p.m., with three-quarters of the wine bottle traveling through my veins and boosting my confidence, I decided to text Oscar. My fingers flew across the screen as I opened the dancers' group chat and selected Oscar's number.

ME

Hey there! My email has been acting up lately and I haven't received the call time for tomorrow. Could you tell me what it is?

Each passing minute felt like an eternity. My mind sped through all the ways he would break the news:

"Oh, you didn't get the email? The one saying you won't be coming in tomorrow?"

"Girl, you really thought you had a job after today?!"

"There is rehearsal tomorrow, but you won't be there."

I spiraled over countless outcomes until... *Bing!* I typed my phone password incorrectly three times before laying my eyes on the text.

> OSCAR
>
> Hey boo. Rehearsal is at 10 a.m. tomorrow.

———

The next day, the same story played out. We warmed up, learned choreography, perfected the steps, and waited hours for Frida to grace us with her presence. The witch shoes tormented another dancer's insteps while my feet recovered inside memory-foam sneakers. The infamous peppermint smell swirled through my nostrils seconds before Frida waltzed in, singing "All That Jazz" as if she'd just teleported from performing the play *Chicago*. Some dancers sang along; others cheered her on. I snapped to the beat, wondering if she'd end the song by announcing my termination. Based on some of the horror stories I'd heard, Frida was more than capable of something like that. But when the finale rolled by, she ended her impromptu performance with jazz hands and a backbend. Then she rose, bowed for applause like a star at the Apollo, and asked Oscar to go over yesterday's choreography.

I waited to get fired for three days, predicting all the different ways they'd break the news, but it never happened. When we wrapped a week later, I couldn't believe I'd cursed at an artist and still managed to finish the job. But folks, don't try this at home.

22

who is this?!

Our sprinter van completed its third circle around the *same* block.

"I think it's official. We're lost," Marvin said as he fumbled with his Sony camera.

"Ha! I hope Letti will be all right without her dancers 'cause we're never gonna get there," I said.

I glanced at the row behind us to find two dancers sound asleep, one with his head slumped forward and the other with hers dangling backward. The hour-long car ride in stop-and-go traffic, accompanied by the powerful AC, provided the perfect conditions to take a pre-show cat nap. Not for Marvin and me, though; we spoke the entire ride. He was a friend of Noah's and offered to get some behind-the-scenes footage of our show. Before today, I'd never met Marvin, but the traffic and our dead phones forced us to get into the nitty-gritty. We shared similarly treacherous stories about past roommates, reminisced about our hometowns, and described how we'd met our partners. Eventually, the conversation veered into the dance industry.

"You said you got into freestyle and hip-hop foundation when you were nineteen," Marvin said. "How was that transition?"

"Scary as hell, but freestyling was scarier. I figured if I focused and kept working hard, eventually it wouldn't be so scary."

"Do you get to work with a lot of freestylers?"

"Sometimes. But most of my jobs are with choreo-heads, and choreo-heads who *swear* they're freestylers."

We threw our heads back in a fit of laughter.

"What do you mean?" Marvin asked in between giggles.

"It's just that, they swear up and down they're freestylers, but they've never trained in a specific style outside of a handful of classes. They've never been in a real cypher or attended a battle. But after those classes and few sessions, they're suddenly a guru, but in reality they're still slaw. Trash with miles to go. It takes years of training for most choreo-heads to be able to learn, retain, and perform choreography well enough to work professionally. I wish they'd show the same care to the freestyle community."

"Ah, I see what you mean. Then they get jobs with their half-assed training."

"Exactly! Half-assed training. Getting famous off it. Teaching watered-down versions, but they can get smoked. Meanwhile, the masters of it—people who devoted their entire lives to it—get lost in history. Silenced too. Because if they say something, people consider them haters or jealous."

"Well, that doesn't make sense," Marvin said. "I've posted a couple of videos where people in my field had no issue letting me know it was grainy or unfocused. It upholds the quality of our art."

"Period! In Florida, freestylers never hesitate to let you know, 'That ain't it.' They'll push you to improve and support you along the way, but you're not safe from critiques."

Our conversation eventually moved to the skill of learning choreography.

"It's crazy how fast some dancers learn. When I used to dance, I couldn't pick up the steps that fast," Marvin said.

"Yeah, now I know several people who can learn sitting down. It's cool, but I feel like it sets unrealistic standards for what a good dancer is. Most jobs have eight-hour rehearsal days. Ample time to pick up the steps."

"Yes, so why pressure dancers to pick up at the speed of light?"

"Right! I don't learn too fast either. I used to be really insecure about it, but the moment I started to get cold at freestyling, all of that changed. Imma get the steps by the time the show comes, and if anyone feels some type of way, they can battle me. That's how I feel."

That sent Marvin into another fit of giggles. "I gotta see you battle one day! I'm sure my boyfriend would love that."

"I don't battle often anymore 'cause dance jobs keep popping up, but if I do end up battling anytime soon, I'll let you know!"

We continued on and on until the lost sprinter-van driver found the back of the arena. I softly woke up the dancers in the back seat, entered the arena, and performed for a sold-out audience.

———

Two weeks later, I received an email from my agent:

Subject: AUDITION for a Tour with a Major Artist

Hello there!

This audition is for a tour with a Major Artist whose name will be disclosed upon booking.

Rate: $2,000 weekly

Rehearsals begin mid-March.

Tour: May to August

Choreographer: Marvin G.

This audition is by invitation only. Do not share!

Please confirm if you will be attending or not.

I closed the email and swiped to the Instagram app on my phone, ready to investigate. I typed "Marvin G." into the search bar and clicked the first account on the list. The profile picture of a body's silhouette in an abstract shape practically screamed dancer. Maybe he did contemporary? But I was wrong. Shocked. His videos were full of hip-hop choreography, but that's not what shocked me. His page made my head spin because I was staring at the same face I'd been stuck in a sprinter van with weeks before.

This was the same person I'd talked to about half-trained choreo-heads faking foundational hip-hop styles. And there he was, on his Instagram with thousands of likes, dancing with the same half-assed training I'd vented to him about. Marvin from the van, the videographer, was Marvin G., the choreographer for this tour. My face, frozen in disbelief, felt ready to slide off my head and onto the floor. *I'm finished. Done.* The industry doesn't take lightly to some of the comments I'd made during that car ride. They can label you as too serious, intense, or problematic for caring about the culture.

After the initial shock wore off, I considered things more deeply. What if he appreciated my view of the industry? Perhaps it was a breath of fresh air compared to the viewpoints he usually heard. Maybe he liked my passionate opinion. Otherwise, he wouldn't have invited me to this audition.

"Marvin G.? Yeah, he's been choreographing for Fulana since 2013," my wife replied after I'd recounted the events in one breath.

She continued, "When I went to Monsters Dance Convention in high school, he was there. He's been in the game for years."

"Great, I'm the only cavewoman that had no clue who he was."

———

A sea of female dancers dressed in black attire sprawled out across the studio. Some stretched. Others caught up with each other. With headphones blasting music to calm my nerves, I stood in the back of the room, rotating my shoulders. My mantra for the day played in my mind alongside the music: *He doesn't hate you. This is an audition you were invited to. You didn't talk out of the side of your neck in the van that day. He understands your love for the craft.*

"Hello, everyone!"

Marvin's entrance halted my body and thoughts. The rest of the room met his arrival with applause.

"Thank you for coming out today. I can't disclose the artist's name, but all you need to know is that this is a big opportunity."

After a couple of minutes, Marvin managed to teach a large, confusing chunk of choreography. The entire room was going down in flames.

"I know I'm teaching fast, but that's on purpose. I need smart dancers. People who can pick up steps and take direction. If you can't do that, you might as well leave now."

I rolled my eyes and continued going over the potpourri of steps in my head. In what felt like the blink of an eye, he'd finished teaching the rest of the routine.

The remainder of the audition was nothing more than

dancers fighting for their lives, doing their best to gain an ounce of stability in this unstable career. All the while, Marvin sprinkled in more tidbits of advice, if one could call it that. Comments that weren't exactly helpful, but not crazy enough to be considered condescending. I was sure of one thing, though: almost every statement he uttered directly contradicted his own talent.

"After the last eight count, freestyle. I shouldn't have to tell a room of professional dancers this, but here it goes: We need strong freestylers. Only the best."

My mind immediately traveled back to his Instagram—a plethora of amazing choreography videos, but none freestyling. Where were his skills at?

"We need style. None of that corny shit."

Yet his videos weren't exactly the pinnacle of originality and fine art.

Every sentence that left his lips hurled me into a deeper state of shock. Who was this person? This couldn't be the same chill, down-to-earth videographer I'd hit it off with in that hour-long car ride, but it was. He'd just been wearing a different hat that day. This professional-choreographer hat must've been three sizes too small and squeezing the worst parts out of him. Whatever he had for breakfast that day must've caused him to turn it up a thousand percent.

Unfortunately, this is something I've experienced too many times in the industry. A humble, sweet person can morph into an entirely different character in a position of power, or in front of a camera or crowd. I'm not sure why people do this. Maybe it's to assert dominance over a room, command respect from those "under them," or uphold a facade. Maybe they turn the focus onto everyone else so that it doesn't fall back on them. I'm not sure. But after Marvin finished teaching that choreography, I grabbed my bags and left. The money didn't matter. I knew for a fact that working under that personality wasn't healthy for me.

23
coping

I fumbled around my purse for some cash while the bartender—and my overpriced tequila sunrise—patiently waited. After the show we'd had, I thought about taking the drink to-go and taking sips while soaking in a hot bath. Instead, I decided to stay put and relax into the barstool as my nightcap hit the spot.

Busted show makeup drooped down my cheeks. Frizz attacked my ponytail extensions. Oversized rehearsal clothes drowned my body, and I had an equally oversized duffel bag with me—an eyesore in this bougie hotel lobby. But the bartender understood. Her long, wavy hair swung back and forth over her name tag, which read "Lianne from Dallas, Texas." A polite woman who had been overly accommodating for the past three nights whenever I purchased some fries or a stiff drink.

Though she hadn't outright said it, Lianne knew we were here for a festival show with Star Monroe, a famous pop artist. Trying her best to contain her excitement and protect my privacy from the other bar patrons, she spoke in code.

"How was tonight?" she asked while mixing another drink order.

"It was great! Beautiful energy from everyone, but I'm excited to go to sleep. Today was a long day. Rewarding, but very long."

After a short pause, Lianne asked, "Is she nice?"

"She's a sweetheart. She works very hard and speaks to everyone in the room, from top to bottom."

"I love to hear that. It's so upsetting when you learn your favorite people aren't good people after all. You have an amazing night, okay?"

"You as well, thank—"

Before I could finish, two tiny hands appeared on my shoulders. When I glanced back, a woman with dilated, bloodshot eyes was staring back at me. She used my body to steady herself as she crouched behind me, her red hair fanned out in different directions.

"Oh! Uh, Star Monroe! How are you?" I repeatedly thanked God that I'd held my tongue earlier.

A smile curved across her face, but she remained silent. My eyes stayed on her while my peripheral vision registered Lianne, who was doing everything possible to keep her cool.

"You must be tired after tonight. Ha, I know I am!" I said.

Star stared back blankly.

Despite my best efforts, even my forced laugh couldn't make this scene less awkward. With her body still tucked behind me like a gargoyle, Star broke our gaze and stared at Lianne.

I quickly scanned the room. Where were her bodyguards? She was never out unprotected. Why was she acting so strange?

"Heyyy honeyyyyy," Star said to Lianne, finally breaking the silence.

"Hey, how's your night going?"

As if she were a schoolgirl, Star snickered and looked back at me, a doll-like smile plastered on her face.

"Youuu, er... did amazing tooonighhht."

"Thank you so much." I turned back toward the bar and unlocked my phone. "You know, I'm so tired, I'm probably going to bed soon. Let me call the tour manager and see if she can come keep you compa—"

And just like that, she was gone, disappearing as quickly as she arrived. Lianne pretended to be busy washing a glass.

"Uh... um...," I stammered.

"Have a great night! I hope you get some rest," Lianne said.

I thanked her, but I was even more grateful that Lianne hadn't addressed what just happened, whatever *that* was. As I walked through the lobby toward the elevators, my eyes searched for Star. My brain, however, replayed everything. By the time I made it to my hotel room, I'd drawn up the only practical reason for Star's behavior that night: she was under the influence of... something.

As a dancer, you'll see parts of an artist most people will never know. Unfortunately, drug use might be one of those parts. I don't condone it, but I don't blame them either. Life on the road is hard. After experiencing the nonstop performing, traveling, and fandom of my first tour, I understand how necessary it is to cope with such a lifestyle. While my coping mechanisms were bubble baths, wine, alone time, and therapy, some people turn to other things like substance abuse.

Find ways to cope with the fast-paced sprints this career can take you through. Practice wholesome self-care activities that will regenerate you; it is vital. Because Star Monroe isn't the only artist out here under the influence.

24
taxes

If you don't need or wish to read about my journey
with taxes, I promise I won't take it personally.
Feel free to skip to the next chapter.

I'll never forget the day my grandmother uttered the words, "Your taxes are too complicated. I can't help you." Mita, my abuela, the resident tax lady in our neighborhood, the only person in my family with tax knowledge, my only resource, couldn't help me.

Because of my first tour, I'd worked in almost all fifty states. Fifty states with different tax laws. After the tour, I booked lots of short-term jobs, such as music videos, teaching gigs, and TV shows. I was hired and fired, and I finished jobs only to be rehired by a different company later. By the end of the year, I had a thick pile of W-2s and 1099s, which at that time I didn't know the difference between.

That was nothing like my abuela's other clients. Jane Doe worked as a schoolteacher all year, and Mami still works at the same nursing job with tax deductions that hardly change. She travels six miles to work and six miles back home, so it's easy to figure out how many miles she drove for work every year. Twelve miles times five days in a week equals sixty miles. Multiply that by fifty work weeks, and you get three thousand miles.

I didn't remember where I rehearsed for that music video back in February. I recalled driving all the way to West LA, but I didn't remember the studio name or the mileage. Until I received that 1099, I didn't even remember taking a weekend trip back in April to teach at a dance studio in Colorado. Because most of my work is short term, it's way more difficult to backtrack at the end of the year.

As soon as they began to arrive in my mailbox, I organized all my W-2s and 1099s into a folder labeled TAXES in big, bold letters. That folder lived on my dresser, patiently waiting for my trip to Florida at the end of March. The timing lined up perfectly with the April 15 tax deadline, not to mention that it saved me the headache of trying to email virtual copies of all the paperwork to a sixty-seven-year-old woman. Leading up to the trip, I prepared as much as I could, saving every piece of mail labeled "End-of-the-Year Tax Document." But nothing prepared me for my abuela's reaction when she opened my folder.

Her eyes widened. It seemed like they got wider with every

page turn. After a couple of pages, she'd squint or shake her head from side to side. Then she delivered the news, the blow to my "well-prepared" heart.

I'll never forget how my feelings snowballed. My abuela dropped the first snowflake out of the sky with the way she reacted. More snowflakes piled on top of it once I realized how soon the tax deadline was. When she told me, "You'll have to find someone else to do it, maybe someone in LA, someone in your industry," the pile of snowflakes collected into a baseball-sized clump.

Someone in my industry? Someone in LA? I moved eight months ago and worked with the same people, who were also not natives, for the majority of those months. I couldn't ask them! As my anxiety escalated, the small snowball inched toward the edge of a mountain cliff.

Before I move forward, I must say that I'm not a tax professional, nor am I able to give tax advice. I advise you to take any questions you might have straight to a trusted tax professional. I'm simply sharing my experience and the things I've learned, and it all began with my introduction to Sheryl.

Though the snowball wavered on the edge, overlooking the fall ahead, it remained steady. I found a tax professional, Sheryl, who had worked with my friend Justice and her family for years. Both Justice and her brother had been working in the entertainment industry since they were kids, so multiple W-2s and short-term jobs were no problem for Sheryl. She knew exactly how to tackle my taxes.

Justice saved the day by connecting me with Sheryl. I

thought she would solve all my issues. But finding a tax professional was only the first step. I was nowhere near prepared for the next one: my tax deductions.

You might be wondering why tax deductions were a problem. For freelancers, independent contractors, and self-employed people, tax deductions are usually an exciting opportunity to save money during tax season. But not for me, at least not during my first couple of years in LA. Instead, deductions were the bane of my existence.

First and foremost, I had no system. No organizational plan to keep track of all my expenses and possible deductions. No recollection of the miles I'd driven to and from jobs all year. Saving receipts for any rehearsal clothes or costumes I purchased? Never heard of such a thing! I wasn't even aware that professional dancers could write off things like hair appointments and makeup purchases since they're crucial for our work. Because I didn't know all of this, searching for these deductions was horrendous.

At the end of each year, I'd scour my home for receipts and endlessly comb through bank statements. And after the whole ordeal was over, all I wanted was to gulp down a big bottle of wine. During the year, that tiny snowball wavered back and forth at the top of the mountain, but at the end of tax season it rampaged down, growing to the size of a three-bedroom home. In the end, I was left with a choice: I'd either find a way to make taxes manageable or be trampled by an avalanche every year.

I tried a lot of things. The "receipts in a shoebox" method was my first attempt, where I saved every physical copy of all my business expenses. I organized the receipts using labeled plastic baggies, but no matter how hard I tried, hundreds of tiny pieces of paper would be overflowing from the shoebox by the end of the year. I was in desperate need of another method.

(I'd like to state that I'm not in paid partnerships with any of the following brands. All my experiences are truthful and influencer-free!)

I had two run-ins with QuickBooks, an accounting software that keeps track of your income, expenses, and much more. QuickBooks allows you to photograph and document receipts, and you can link your business bank account to categorize expenses. It's so popular that many professional accountants and bookkeepers work exclusively with this software.

Perhaps I didn't take enough time to tailor this software to my business, but I had so much trouble finding categories for my expenses. How was I supposed to categorize a $450 payment for headshots or a $680 union fee for SAG-AFTRA? Tons of online tutorials promised to help me customize QuickBooks, but during my two experiences, I didn't have the capacity to learn. Therefore, I became less and less active, until several months had passed since I'd last logged on. Meanwhile, subscription payments continued to leave my account.

After canceling my subscription, I discovered another bookkeeping software called FreshBooks. It was like QuickBooks but it was more affordable, the learning curve wasn't as steep, and I could immediately begin customizing the site for my business. FreshBooks felt like a match made in heaven, a relationship I thought would last forever—until COVID-19 hit.

For many of us, the pandemic caused uncertainty and financial strife. For weeks, the entertainment industry stood at a standstill. No income poured into my household. In order to survive, my wife and I had to save money and cut expenses as much as possible. My FreshBooks subscription was one of the first to go. Though my spirit was convinced that FreshBooks was the end-all-be-all, I didn't take the loss too hard. Decisions had to be made. I had to adapt, which led me to my current method.

The Numbers app is a free software for Apple products. By way of iCloud, the app can sync up with all your devices, making it easy to update on the go. It's almost identical to Microsoft Excel, and in the midst of the pandemic, anything free was for me.

Every year, I construct a file for each month—for example, March 2020, April 2020. Inside each file, I create five tabs: "Mileage," "Income," "Bills," "Expenses," and "Summary." And inside each tab are charts personalized to my specific line of work.

In the following paragraphs, I'll break down my process, separated by the five tabs I use.

1. mileage

A list of all the destinations I drive to for work.

The columns in this chart are labeled "Date," "Job Description," "From," "To," and "Miles." We do a lot of different things for dance jobs, so the mileage doesn't just include traveling between home and rehearsal. For example, we might have to drive to West LA to take a COVID test, drive to a location in Hollywood for rehearsal, and then drive to a set in Santa Clarita for the shoot day.

In the "From" and "To" columns, I write out the full address of each location. I can then calculate the mileage using any GPS app. I also have a row that shows the total number of miles I drive each month. I used to save gas station receipts, but according to Sheryl, the IRS prefers mileage. (Once again, don't take this information as law. Always fact-check with your own tax professional!)

2.   income

The money I make each month.

This tab has four columns: "Job," "Amount," "Gross Pay," and "Job Type." I try to be as specific as possible in each column. For example, the job might be *The Great Lane*, Episode 204, choreographed by Rhapsody, with an amount of $1,687.23, a gross pay of $2,290.34 and a W-2 job type.

To avoid helplessly searching through emails later, it's vital to be as specific as possible from the get-go. I've had trouble booking my tax appointments in the past. From January to March, countless W-2s and 1099s are mailed to my home. Because I never kept track of how many W-2 and 1099 jobs I did, I had no way to know how many letters to expect in the mail. So when the mail slowed down at the end of tax season, I figured all the documents had made it, and I'd book my appointments with Sheryl. But fears would float quietly in the back of my mind:

Am I missing any forms?

Will one arrive in the mail after it's too late?

Will the IRS audit me for unclaimed money?

Nevertheless, I continued to my appointments with fear looming in the background. Nowadays, that fear is completely eradicated. The "Job Type" column makes it easy for me to tally up how many W-2 and 1099 jobs I did.

3. bills

Recurring monthly payments.

General bills include rent/mortgage, the car note, insurance, electricity, gas, phone, and internet. If you have a home office, you might be able to incorporate those expenses into your deductions. Electricity keeps the lights on for you to work. The phone and internet are necessary for your work to be completed. Always run it by your tax professional first, but if it's essential for your business, it could be a valid deduction.

Keep in mind that I have many different streams of income. I have my dance work, which includes teaching and commercial work. I work with different brands on social media. Then I have my brand and e-commerce store. And last but not least, I work a part-time virtual administration job for a therapist. Here are some of the other recurring monthly expenses and not-so-obvious bills for my businesses:

- ProWritingAid: a grammar and spellcheck editing software
- Adobe Lightroom: photo-editing for author promo, dance headshots, and clothing promo

- Apple Music: for teaching, filming self-taped auditions, and content creation
- Canva: for photo-editing, flyers, and social media content
- Microsoft Word: a writing and editing software
- Dropbox: for document storage
- Shopify: for my e-commerce business
- GoDaddy: for my personal website

4.   expenses

One-time or infrequent payments.

In my organizational system, expenses are different from bills in that expenses don't recur monthly. They're transactions that happen only once or a couple of times throughout the year. This tab isn't to document the seventy-eight dollars you spent on dog food this month; instead, all expenses should be a necessary part of running your business. Here are some of mine:

- Laptop purchase
- Car repairs
- Home repairs
- Printer purchase, including ink and repairs

- Vellum, a book-editing software
- Book cover designer
- Book editor
- Purchases for the home office, like a desk or a computer chair
- Also consider including medical expenses:
- Co-pays (dental, primary doctor, optometrist, therapist, etc.)
- Prescription eyeglasses
- Contact lenses
- Emergency and urgent care

I'm a dancer, my body is my instrument. Therefore, that allows me to claim certain expenses that help keep this instrument running, such as physical therapy, acupuncture, massage therapy, cryotherapy, and gym memberships.

That being said, your expenses have to be within reason. For example, I schedule bodywork once or twice a month, depending on my schedule. These treatments keep my body healthy, promote recovery, and prepare me for my next job. But if I tried to write off a ninety-dollar massage for every day of the year, that might be harder to justify to the IRS.

For dancers and other performing artists, our bodies are not only our instruments, but our brands. Casting directors hire us based on our brands and what we bring to the table, which includes our looks. They might need a white Latina and an Afro–Latina for a Spanish phone commercial. They might need a plus-size mixed or ethnically ambiguous woman for a clothing print ad. As shallow as it might sound, in the commercial world, your look is your brand. Looks and talent get you hired; therefore, you may have to make purchases to maintain your looks.

Here are some dancer-specific purchases I include in my expenses (within reason, of course):

- Makeup
- Haircuts and hair products
- Skin treatments, like facials and laser hair removal
- Nail salon visits: I don't get my nails done, but I know quite a few dancers who do and include this in their expenses. Gotta be presentable for auditions!
- Headshots: This is a really important write-off because headshots are typically a very high expense— anywhere from two hundred to eight hundred dollars. They're also of the utmost importance. Without a headshot, a casting director, agent, or choreographer might not even consider you, whether you're talented or not.

To keep up the necessary talent and skills to be a dancer, I also include any money I spend on classes and courses.

If you're unsure about what qualifies as an expense or not, keep track of every purchase that could be an expense and then present them all to your tax professional. They'll let you know what you can and can't write off, like that clay you purchased for your pottery hobby.

5. summary

A general overview of your finances for that month.

This tab shows the entirety of the data I entered in the previous tabs. I use it to see how well I did that month. I label the columns as follows:

- Income
- Bills
- Expenses
- Amount in Personal Checking Account(s)
- Amount in Personal Savings Account(s)
- Amount in Business Account(s)
- Credit Card Debt
- Debt in General

With these columns, you're able to look at every facet of your financial health at once. If your total income was $5,600 that month, and your bills and expenses totaled $8,000, you can assess and create a game plan. By comparing your monthly summary pages, you can track decreasing or increasing debt. If you ended the month with too little in your accounts, you can construct a plan to rectify that the following month. Some people prefer charts, but seeing the exact numbers side by side helps me the most.

Over time, I've noticed more and more dancers doing their own taxes. I don't judge or look down on this in any way, but I know myself. I don't have the capacity to learn this trade and keep up with ever-changing tax laws, so I have no problem hiring a professional to do it for me.

There are tons of automated programs that can help you keep track of everything listed above. However, if you prefer a human's eye, you could hire a bookkeeper to organize it all. I adopted my system using the Numbers app to save money during the pandemic. I loved FreshBooks, so I wasn't particularly happy about the change at first, but then I fell in love with it. And it was for FREE!

When it comes to taxes, find what works for you and always seek professional help.

25

the hdigh tour

Congratulations! You made it through a long, boring chapter about taxes!... Or you skipped it... Now let's get to some more tea, this time from a part of my life I jokingly call the "Dark Ages"—the years before I was with my wife.

I like to describe this particular tour with one phrase: "How did I get here?" I call it the HDIGH Tour for short. (Most of the time, it felt more like the "How the *fuck* did I get here?!" Tour, but to keep it cute, we'll leave the profanity out of it.)

This tour launched me into a cyclone of experiences. A series of exhilarating and somewhat traumatic events that taught me some of my most important life lessons.

Early adulthood is an explorative time. These are the years most young adults spend finding themselves in college—a world where most of its inhabitants are on the same journey. Being on a national tour as during this stage of life is *very* different.

On the HDIGH Tour, the ages were all over the place. The stagehands and truck drivers were generally forty and up, production held the middle spot between thirty and forty, and the dancers were as young as eighteen to around thirty-five.

The HDIGH Tour was crazy for multiple reasons. First off, I had two crushes. Two smitten, middle-school-like, lost-for-words-but-trying-with-all-my-might-to-act-normal crushes.

Marley was the first one. As soon as rehearsals started, I was in awe. Marley was hands down one of the strongest dancers. Because of her background in cheerleading and tumbling, she could perform several flips without an ounce of hesitation. Even if she was nervous or scared, she never backed down from a challenge. Marley was the first person I'd ever seen land a kip-up in heels.

One thing about me—I love women who are phenomenal at what they do. It's kind of a weakness of mine. Even if your looks or personality didn't reel me in, your talent can easily seal the deal. That's what happened with Marley.

I wouldn't consider myself prejudiced, but the truth is, I'd never had a crush on a white person before this moment. Paul Walker and Rachel McAdams slipped through the cracks, but they were the only two on the list.

When magazines and tabloids highlighted the most beautiful women in the industry, I sometimes had trouble understanding their choices. When I was a teen, for the life of me, I couldn't understand the hype around Angelina Jolie's lips. The novelty of them. At that time it wasn't common for white women to have such naturally big lips, but I'd seen black women and Latinas with lips like that my whole life, so hers didn't stand out.

Growing up, my culture praised wide hips and full bodies. Back then, the rest of the world—predominately led by white beauty standards—was still living by the mantra "the skinnier, the better." The things I loved about women weren't common in white women at that time, so I guess I never looked in their direction.

Until Marley, a white girl from Charlotte, North Carolina. During our first week of rehearsals, she performed all the strenuous parts of the routines with ease. The muscles in her legs and back supported her through the long workdays. But when I watched her land that kip-up in those high heels on her first try, she could've had *all* my lunch money.

SHE and I were just close friends at the time, so she was the first to hear about my crush. We called her "Marley the Unicorn." SHE would tease and try to convince me to flirt, but I was too scared, especially when Marley became my roommate for the six-month-long tour. I didn't want her to feel uncomfortable in any way, shape, or form, so I shelved that crush and tried my best to be a girl's girl. The regular, platonic girlfriend she could gossip to after rehearsals and kill bottles of wine with. That's it.

By placing that crush on the back burner, I think I unknowingly made room for a new one. Rosa, the spicy Puerto Rican girl from New York, was also a beast in her craft. When the job began, I clicked with Rosa almost immediately. We bonded over our shared Puerto Rican culture and similar senses of humor.

The rest of the cast would always find us together, like two peas in a pod.

My crush on Rosa developed toward the end of rehearsals. The flame started when I noticed how touchy and hands-on she was. For some reason, a lot of female dancers are touchy, invading your personal bubble even when they're talking about regular subjects that don't require so much closeness. During a fit of giggles, they might place their hand on your thigh or lay out on your lap completely.

On the surface, this all seemed like regular girl behavior to me: sleeping over, sharing beds, sharing secrets under the covers, just like in all those iconic girls' movies. I used to love that stuff—uninterrupted girl time in the midst of this patriarchal world. But at thirteen, when a friend's hand on my thigh evolved into full make-out sessions, it changed my perception of "girl time" forever.

To this day, I stiffen up and think twice when women invade my personal bubble. Of course, I have friends I can break that bubble with, holding hands and hugging for a long time, but these are women I've known for years. Our relationships have evolved. They didn't start out that way or spring up out of nowhere.

Rosa maintained a good balance. She wasn't overly invasive, but she still broke my bubble from time to time. I guess I was too engulfed in my crush on Marley to think about Rosa as more than a friend. That is, until she became my shower buddy.

The HDIGH Tour was wild—not only because I had to deal with college-aged hormones on my first professional job, but also because more than seventy shows were scheduled over four months. Since it was a bus tour, we had to get off stage and head to the next city as soon as possible.

If we finished the show at 10:30 p.m., bus call was at midnight. That left us with no time for extracurricular activities. We only went clubbing when the next city wasn't too far away. On these days, the production team granted us a bus call of 2 a.m. or 3 a.m., giving us free time to explore that city's nightlife.

But on a regular show day, free time was scarce. Call times were soon after the show ended, and because most of the theaters were small, there would only be two to five showers available at a time. For a crew of about thirty people.

Because the consensus among camps is that dancers are children, production saw no issue in suggesting that we partner up for showers to use our time more effectively. Yes, the production team, crew members, and drivers all deserved their own showers, but dancers could sacrifice theirs. The male dancers, a group made up of mostly gay men and two straight men, also opted out of the shared showers, leaving only the female dancers.

Nowadays, I'd meet a suggestion like that with a blunt "Hell no." But it was one of my first jobs, and back then I didn't know any better. So my focus immediately shifted to whom I'd select to be my shower buddy.

Anybody but Marley, the little voice inside my head pleaded. *That's too much for me to handle. Please, anyone but her.*

I'm not sure if she heard my silent prayer or thought it could work 'cause of our close friendship, but Rosa chose me. And that's when things began to unravel.

I always noticed Rosa's ass. That's a friendly thing women do. It's completely normal to look at another woman's ass and say, "Girl, those jeans make your butt look great." I can cross that line without any overwhelming gay feelings, pointing out the many things that make women beautiful without lusting after them, and I've always been proud of that.

Until I saw Rosa undress for the first time.

Excitement buzzed around the dressing room after we'd finished our first show on the tour. We exchanged congratulatory hugs and high fives until reality set in: Bus call was in an hour and a half. We had to get with our buddies and shower quickly or be forced to sleep on the bus covered in dried sweat until we arrived at the next city.

Rosa wasted no time. "Come on, Yoe! Let's go!"

"Bitch, hold on!" I laughed, scrambling for my shower sandals and soap.

Seconds later, we were in the restroom, undressing as the shower ran.

"I can't believe we did the first show," Rosa said.

We were in our bras and underwear.

"Crazy, right? Rehearsals were so long. I was getting tired of that all-black dance studio. I felt like I was about to lose my mind in there."

"Right! Especially 'cause of all the times we ran the show. The repetition was killing me!"

She pulled her hair into a messy bun on top of her head.

"Me too! Those rehearsals were hard."

I turned toward the shower and made sure the water was

warm before getting fully undressed. It wasn't; it was hot. Borderline *too* hot, just how I liked it. Satisfied, I unclipped my bra, turned around to set it with my things, and then saw Rosa was already naked.

All the tight, formfitting clothing she'd worn in rehearsal did her no justice. The leggings, spandex shorts, sports bras—none of it did. Seeing her without anything on made me realize her figure was practically *perfect.*

Sweat immediately formed in my armpits. I can't tell you what we talked about while we were in the shower 'cause I was secretly having a panic attack. It was as if two versions of me were functioning at the same time. The outside Yoe spoke, laughed, and asked questions like, "Okay are you ready for the water now?" But the Yoe inside was watching the platonic-friend zone evaporate like water during a drought. It disappeared and was replaced by lust. For the rest of our shower, I inhaled deep calming breaths and tried to snap out of it.

This went on for the first week we were on the road. I consider this the real beginning of the HDIGH Tour, 'cause how did I end up on a tour taking a shower with someone *this* fine?!

Prior to the tour, I'd had a boyfriend for a few months. He was a nice guy. I wanted to take some time to explore men because I'd mostly dealt with women before him. When conversations about our dating lives sprang up, Rosa and I had only talked about my ex-boyfriend, so she had no clue about my past experiences with women. I felt like a dormant volcano that was slowly awakening.

After that first week on tour, the strong feelings for my

shower buddy faded. They didn't disappear because she was any less fine or because Marley had finally professed her love to me. No, my crush faded because on our first day off, after completing five demanding show days in a row, I drunkenly slept with one of the male dancers.

How the fuck did *that* happen?!

26

lock the door

There we were, in the back of the tour bus en route to the next city, opening our second bottle of Moscato. We were singing at the top of our lungs to a playlist that had a little bit of everything, from Miley Cyrus's "Party in the U.S.A." to Eve's "Let Me Blow Ya Mind."

After five days of back-to-back shows in five different cities, we finally had an off day. In the morning we'd be arriving in New Orleans and checking into a hotel. Sharing a hotel room with one person would be a luxurious vacation compared to sharing a bus with eight dancers. It was a much-needed break we desperately looked forward to.

After every show, we kept it cute. A handful of us remained in the front of the bus, watched some TV, had a glass of wine, and then retreated to our bunks to rest for the next day's show.

But because we had a day off the next day, that handful of

people watching TV transformed into a party with all twelve of us packed in the bus's back lounge. Those single glasses of wine evolved into us killing an entire bottle and us popping open another. Eventually we finished that bottle too.

In a space that comfortably fit about six people, twelve of us were scattered across the couch and the tables, standing around and bracing for any sharp turns or hard brakes the bus driver might make. We sang, danced, and partied. Because of the tight space, our bodies were close, and I secretly melted every time Rosa or Marley brushed against me.

At some point everyone was passing around a bottle of Jack Daniel's and waterfalling shots into their mouths. Even though I was nineteen, I knew the rule: No mixing. "Beer before liquor, never been sicker." But I'd never heard anything about *wine* before liquor! Not to mention that the two bottles of Moscato we'd killed off had given me a dangerous amount of liquid courage. So, when they passed that bottle around for the first, second, and fifth time, I didn't say no.

It wasn't long before I couldn't tell if the bus was moving or not. The entire space around me was spinning. At first, excitement circulated in that tiny back lounge. Now drunken karaoke and lots of twerking were sprinkled into the mix.

Then one of my favorite club songs, "One Minute Man," came on. As soon as that infamous beat hit my ears, I started winding my hips to the music. The door to the back lounge was closed, so I started dancing in front of it like it was a person, changing my levels, going from low to high, performing some full-out syncopated ass shaking...

Suddenly the cold, flat feeling of the lounge door behind me disappeared and was replaced with a warm body. When I turned around, I was surprised to see Vic, one of the only two straight males on the tour. Prior to this night, Vic and I had never been so close. We'd had small talk here and there during rehearsals, and we'd attended group outings together, but that was about it.

Now here he was, pushing up on me to one of my favorite songs. I looked back at him and thought, *Huh? Shit, oh well!* Liquid courage took over all my thoughts and transported me back to my teen club days. My thirteen-year-old self wildly cheered me on:

Ooooo, he must not know who you are!

You used to have the boys AND the girls hurtin' at the teen club!

He gon' find out tonight!

With the support of my drunk alter ego, I kept dancing on Vic. Even when the song ended and the next song played, I kept going. Then that song ended. And the song after that. With each song, the intensity of my hips increased, and so did his desire beneath me.

When we first started dancing, everyone cheered, "Wooo! Okay, Yoe!" They supported the dance as if it were a moment in the party. Little did I know that this dance would be the end of the night. As the music kept on playing and the intensity between Vic and me increased, the other dancers excused themselves one by one from the back lounge. I'm not sure when or how it happened, but in what felt like a flash, Vic and I were the only people left in the back lounge, the music still going, both of us still dancing.

Keeping my hips steadily on his, he shifted us to the couch. And with another club song filling the speakers, he sat down facing the door. My hips stuck to his like glue. Our standing dance had morphed into a lap dance.

Vic's hands explored my body. Our breaths became short and labored.

For a moment I thought, *I should stop. This is going to go too f—*

"Go lock the door," Vic said, interrupting my thoughts.

As if a witch had me under a spell, everything stopped—the winding in my hips, the second thoughts in my head. I just got up and locked the door. All while periodically thinking, *How the fuck did I get here?!*

Dear reader, if you're on tour, don't have sex in the front or back lounge of the bus. These are spaces for EVERYONE. Yuck! Oh, and try not to get plastered on your first off day.

27

fuzzy

The next morning at 8 a.m., the tour bus parked on a busy street in Washington, DC, in front of a hotel.

"All right, everyone, wake up! The bus can't stay here, so grab what you need and check into the hotel. If you forget something, you can text the tour manager for the address the bus is parked at."

The bus driver's announcement sounded like nails on a chalkboard. A throbbing headache pounded my brain as I stumbled around, grabbing my belongings from the bunk. With my tote bag in one arm and my toiletry bag in the other, I was ready to get off and retrieve my luggage from the storage compartment under the bus. I took a step forward and tripped over a shoe someone had left in the middle of the hallway. Judging by how loud the music in the back lounge had been the night before and the empty bottles scattered everywhere, I'm sure the bus driver knew *exactly* why we were struggling to move around.

As I tripped, a hat—which I had no clue was on my head—fell onto the floor. A green hat. My fuzzy, still-drunk brain tried to make sense of it all.

I don't even own a green...

Ohhh.

Images of me sitting on Vic's lap while he grabbed my neck flashed through my mind. I ignored the uneasy feeling in the pit of my stomach.

This is Vic's hat. Where is...?

The sound of someone vomiting interrupted my thoughts. I looked toward the front of the bus to see Vic on his knees inches away from the exit, throwing up into a small trash can. His duffel bag was on the floor next to him, like he was just about to get off the bus when his stomach turned on him. Probably because of the mix of Moscato and Jack Daniel's from last night.

My stomach lurched at the sight of Vic's head in the trash can. To avoid two people vomiting on the bus, I fast-walked past Vic, gently placing the hat on his head on my way out. I clumsily pulled my two large suitcases out from under the bus and dragged them into the hotel.

As soon as I walked into my hotel room, I left my luggage by the door and jumped straight into bed. All I could think was, *WTF happened last night, Yoe?!*

Scene by scene, blurry visions of the previous night played in my head: Moscato, Jack Daniel's, a whole bunch of sexual tension, and Vic's body against mine. The events replayed multiple times before I finally came to grips with what happened.

I had sex with Vic last night.

WHAT, Yoe?

I was disappointed in myself for sleeping with this man I barely knew, in the back lounge of a bus, with the rest of my coworkers a couple of feet away—more importantly, when I was a couple of feet away from two coworkers I would've *rather* been intimate with.

That was upsetting, but it didn't alarm me. What alarmed me was—no matter how many times I replayed the moments when I got up, locked the door, and guided Vic inside of me—I couldn't for the life of me remember a condom.

Did he have one? Did he slip it on quickly? What the hell happened after he came? Oh, yeah, he passed out.

All I remembered was getting up, pulling his pants up, and leaving him passed out in the back lounge. Then I went to the front of the bus, used the restroom, and went to sleep. After repeatedly playing back this drunken memory, I accepted reality: we didn't use a condom.

Folks, *always* use protection, especially with people you barely know.

28
two out of six

My fingers were moving at the speed of light.

ME

Fren…

ROSA

What?

ME

Last night… was crazy…

ROSA

Yeah… Last night was… a lot. I have to
tell you something.

*Huh? I have to tell her something. What does she have to
tell me?*

I thought I'd locked the door, but maybe I didn't. Maybe Rosa opened it and saw me having sex with Vic. Or maybe before having sex with Vic, I made some drunken gay pass at her and now she felt weird. In a perfect world, we would've hooked up and this text would've been to meet up to do it again. *UGH!*

I took a long, deep breath before replying.

ME

What happened?

ROSA

There's two things…

ME

Rosa. Come on!

ROSA

So Leo and I have been hooking up since the second week of rehearsals. But last night, we had sex in the front lounge and we didn't use protection.

My hungover headache rang like a school bell. That single text dismantled any ounce of a crush I had left, deflated my heart, and brought me back to my own issues.

ME

WTF?! What is going on? 1. I can't believe I didn't pick up on that. 2. You won't believe what happened to me last night.

ROSA

WHAT!

ME

I had sex with Vic in the back lounge and I was too drunk to remember if we used a condom or not.

ROSA

ARE YOU SERIOUS?! I saw y'all dancing for one song, but me and Leo left to the front! This is crazy.

Crazy was right. There were very few straight men on tour, and we ran through two of them in one night. Well, I guess over multiple nights, in Rosa's case.

ME

Bitch, yes... I just got into my room. I'm gonna wash my face, brush my teeth, and go to the pharmacy and get a Plan B.

ROSA

Okay, let me know when you get back. Let's go get some food.

ME

HUH?! You just told me you didn't use a condom last night either. WE are gonna go get Plan B. So be ready in ten.

After years of being sexually active with women only, and then having a boyfriend for a short time but still feeling like a lesbian, this is where I ended up. Sulking, wanting to disappear, as I walked into the pharmacy and whispered to the woman at the counter, "Can I have a Plan B?"

(Though I was young and traumatized, I realize now that there's no shame in purchasing Plan B. This is a responsible decision, and don't let society slut-shame you.)

So, yeah. I went through all of that, and I didn't even come.

How? Did? I? Get? Here?

29

the morning after

After a trip to the pharmacy that I'll never forget, Rosa and I ended up at a breakfast spot with some of the other dancers.

I searched the menu, desperately looking for something fluffy and full of bread to cure my hangover. Then it jumped out at me: a picture of thick-cut French toast with powdered sugar and fruit layered on top. Perfect. That's it. My search had come to an end.

Feeling one step closer to recovery, I lowered my menu and locked eyes with Vic.

My mind flashed back to the group text I'd gotten while waiting in line at the pharmacy.

> Breakfast at 10 a.m. for those who
> wanna come!

But why did I come here?

I couldn't fully comprehend the message 'cause I'd been dealing with a sea of other thoughts at the time. But here were Vic and Leo, strolling into the brunch spot, looking kind of tired but also refreshed. Everyone looked refreshed, like they'd had time to shower, put on fresh fits, and even shave or put on some makeup. Meanwhile, Rosa and I had thrown our bags into our hotel rooms, brushed our teeth, washed our faces, and taken a guilt-ridden field trip to the pharmacy.

One by one, Leo and Vic greeted everyone at the table with a handshake. My heart skipped several beats as he inched closer and closer to me.

"What's good, Yoe?"

"Nothing much. Tired as hell!" My hand trembled as he shook it.

"Me too. I don't remember what time I went to sleep, but it must've been late."

Memories from the night rushed through my mind like a three-second timelapse. "Yeah, I think I got four hours of sleep."

He laughed and then moved on to greet the remaining dancers. I felt the tension release from my shoulders a little bit.

Whew, okay. He didn't seem awkward about it. Maybe he doesn't feel awkward. Or maybe he's just playing it off. Maybe he thinks we're in a relationship now?! Ugh. That would be a tourmance born from a huge mistake. Maybe he expects more tonight in the privacy of a hotel room. Maybe he—

"And what would you like to eat?" the young, bright-eyed waitress in front of me said, pausing my spiraling thoughts.

———

With bellies full of food and coffee, we poured out of the restaurant and found ourselves in Washington, DC, a city most of us had never explored. Side conversations buzzed all around. Some dancers talked about visiting monuments. Others talked about shopping. Rosa and I spoke to each other without words. We exchanged looks that screamed, "Let's go back to the hotel and take a nap."

My full stomach, lack of sleep, and the alcohol still leaving my body screamed, REST. *Mentally prepare for your show tomorrow and figure out how the hell you're going to finish this six-month-long tour after having slept with Vic.*

"Where you heading?" Vic said, interrupting my thoughts.

"Uh, nowhere. I'll probably just rest today. I still feel a little crazy from last night."

"Yeah, I still feel a little crazy too." He paused as if he were going to finally break the ice about what we did. I searched his eyes for something. Anything. Then laughter erupted from his belly. "But I threw most of it up this morning. Haha!"

I squeezed forced laughter through my lips. "Yeah, I'm gonna drink a lot of water before I go to sleep."

As quickly as it had begun, our talk ended. Vic moved on to have another random conversation. Not only did he avoid speaking about the previous night, but he didn't even *hint* at it. Everything about him, from his demeanor to his gaze, was bland. Friendly. This wasn't the person who'd whispered "Go lock the door" in my ear late last night.

Maybe he knew it was a mistake. For me, the mistake was sleeping with my coworker—and with another man in general. After trying it with my ex, I'd decided to give it a break and go back to what I knew. Women. Divine feminine energy. What I was used to. But somehow, with the help of lots of alcohol, I'd added a second male to my body count.

For him, the mistake was sleeping with his coworker—or anyone at all for that matter, since he was engaged. Though I'd never met his fiancée, I'd seen all their pictures on social media and overheard him speaking to her on Facetime during rehearsal breaks. He was probably going through just as much turmoil as me, if not more. That's why he didn't even mention it. That's why he acted like nothing happened.

Yeah, that's it. We're gonna act like nothing happened.

A part of me was relieved. Hell, I preferred to bury it so far in my memory that it'd never see the light of day again. I thought if I suppressed it, maybe all these feelings would go with it: Guilt for sleeping with an engaged man. Crippling embarrassment from buying my first Plan B. Shame because I couldn't remember where the deed was finished. And lastly, regret. If I'd slept with anyone on tour, I really wanted it to be Marley or Rosa —not Vic! He'd never even made it on my radar before our little excursion. So why, God? Why?

My dear reader, if a tourmance does bud for you, don't be like me. TALK, TALK, TALK about it!

30

oceanside

Even after two weeks had passed, Vic never brought up that night. He acted completely normal. He was friendly, but it was the same kind of friendliness he showed everyone else. I looked out for secretive glances and hidden meanings in our short conversations, but they never surfaced.

Wow, it's really behind us, I thought. *We're on some grown shit. We did this and never have to talk about it or do it again. Is this what adults do? 'Cause I like it!*

I didn't want to make a habit of this behavior, but in my eyes, this was the perfect solution for my huge blunder.

Then we found ourselves in Miami. Though it's a little livelier and more populated than Tampa, it reminds me of my hometown all the same. Caribbean accents fill the air, familiar foods can be found on every corner, and the ocean is never too far away.

Since that fateful night with Vic, we'd only had one more off day in some small town I can't even remember. I spent most of that day annihilating a bottle of Moscato with Rosa while she stressed about her budding feelings for Leo. After learning they'd been an unofficial item since rehearsals, my crush disappeared. I wasn't a fan of possibly sharing her with anyone, and I couldn't share her even if I wanted to. Rosa was straight. I'd never had a chance. After the initial blow, I was fine. And as the months passed, I was glad to have such a close friend on the tour and thankful that I hadn't slept with her.

"Okay, bitch! We are *not* stressin' over your feelings for Leo in this city," I said. "We're taking a break from that and living our fullest lives in Miami. We have TWO days off. Not one, but TWO. Salsa clubs, bomb-ass Cuban food, and ocean water will be the only things on our agenda!"

I was slathering lotion all over my arms and scanning my outfit in the mirror. After changing multiple times, I'd ended up in a lace crop top and denim cargo pants. Cute and still comfortable enough to dance in.

"Ugh, okay. But what if he texts me?"

"Sis, we have three and a half months of this tour left. There will be enough time to smash!"

"That's not the only thing I want, though. I wanna talk. I like when we talk. We can literally talk about anything."

"Oop, there you go falling in love again."

"I can't call it love. That would be crazy. Let's say *overwhelmed*. These feelings for him overwhelm me sometimes!"

"All right. Like I said, we're pausing on that for one night 'cause we're in Miami. The only thing that's gonna overwhelm us is the sound of live Latin music."

All the dancers, some of the crew members, the music engineer, and even the lighting director took Miami by storm. We started the night with magical Cuban food. After walking off our food babies on Ocean Drive, we floated into a salsa club. Then we ended up at a hip-hop bar where we had multiple shots of whatever the bartender gave us. Our large group gave the otherwise drab space the energy it needed, and the bartender enjoyed it. He gifted us several rounds that were either discounted or on the house. The best part was he didn't card the underage members of the crew, myself included.

Though Vic and Leo were there, I never felt strange. I spent most of my time partying with the ladies and fake ballroom dancing with the gay male dancers like we were on *Dancing with the Stars*.

We stumbled out of the club at around 2 a.m. and headed back to the hotel.

"If y'all still down to hang, I got some games in my room!" I yelled to the group. "Room 1615!"

They roared back with different responses:

"Okay, lemme take off this itchy dress!"

"All right, I'll get another bottle!"

"I'm gonna kill my leftovers, then I'll be up there!"

"Perfect, let's meet in my room at three," I said. "That gives me enough time to shower real quick. I smell like a walking Cuban cigar!"

After one of the quickest showers known to mankind, I

changed into sweats and a t-shirt, placed three board games on the table, and lit a candle. I opened my balcony curtains and let the view serve as real-life art. For miles, the ocean was the only thing in sight, with moonlight cascading over the crashing waves. The camp had really spoiled us by choosing this hotel on the beach.

By 3:30 a.m. I was sitting on my balcony, sipping Moscato and scrolling through my phone. The relaxing ocean sounds unwound my body and prepared me for the likely event that no one would be coming to my room for games. I'd only taken two shots at the bar, but I'd seen some dancers take five. Rosa messaged me as soon as she made it to her room.

ROSA

Fren, I'm going to sleep. I just puked my brains out.

Other dancers had probably shared the same fate.

I lifted my glass for another sip when I heard a knock on the door.

"Oh! Uh, hey!" I stammered when I saw Vic standing in the doorway.

He chuckled when he noticed the silence in my room. "I guess everybody turned it in?"

"Shoot, I guess the free shots caught up with everyone."

"Yeah, I went to Leo's room and he was giving the shots back to his toilet."

"That's crazy 'cause Rosa texted me the same thing."

He lifted a plastic bag filled with Jack Daniel's, ginger ale, and lemon juice. "Since the rest of the crew is probably fighting for their lives, I'm not gonna keep you up. But can I make you my signature drink?"

Nerves crept through my stomach. "Sure!"

We sat on my balcony while I sipped a perfectly crafted drink. Refreshing, sweet, but nowhere near as sugary as the Moscato I'd been drinking. Shuffled music played through my portable speaker.

"This drink is amazing."

"Thanks, I learned how to make it in college. Can't be taking shots all the time. It's too strong."

That sentence returned my brain to reality. The shots of vodka at the bar, the glass of Moscato, and the Jack Daniel's concoction were a mixing disaster waiting to happen. Just like that one night...

"I need to slow down before I end up like Leo and Rosa."

"No, I saw Leo. He takes the win for tonight."

I laughed. "Yeah, but I've been sitting this whole time. You know things feel different when you stand!"

"Try standing."

I stood up and felt a sensation rushing to my feet. Besides the alcohol weighing down my legs, I didn't feel nauseous or dizzy, which was a victory in my book.

"Yes!" I jumped up and down. "I'm not dizzy. Maybe I won't end up sick!"

"Lemme see." He got up, and we stood side by side facing the dark waves crashing against the shore. "I feel fine too. But I didn't have too many shots at the bar."

"Yeah, me—Oooohhh! This is my song!"

Eve's "Let Me Blow Ya Mind" played through the tiny speaker. Over my loud rapping and the distant ocean sounds, I could hear Vic laughing at my performance. My hips rocked from side to side while I closed my eyes and pictured myself on stage with Eve herself. In this tipsy moment, no one could tell me otherwise. I wasn't just on stage with Eve, I *was* Eve! I was the award-winning performer, hitting all the lyrics with perfect...

What is that?

I felt a warm body nuzzle up behind me, working his hips with mine. We were no longer standing side by side on the balcony. The balcony wall, me, and Vic were sandwiched together, with little space in front of me and none behind me. Every inch—behind my hips, my back, and my neck—Vic had invaded. The deepest part of my stomach stirred, but I never stopped singing or dancing. And he joined in, singing the lyrics softly in my ear.

Before I knew it, my dancing had intensified—no longer a soft rock from side to side, but a full-blown grind into Vic. The song ended and our singing stopped, but we kept moving. The more my hips pushed back, the more his moved forward. He kept his mouth near my ear, but instead of singing, short breaths left his mouth, matching the air skipping in my lungs.

I couldn't tell you what song was playing on this balcony 'cause a few minutes later, my pants were around my ankles as we performed a *different* dance. Overlooking the beach in

Miami, I almost reached my peak, but Vic pulled out and released on my backside.

"Damn, you made me cum quick."

"It's okay," I said almost automatically. I rarely climaxed with my ex, so I figured this was common when dealing with men.

After wiping off, we returned to our chairs. I sipped my drink and stared at the water ahead.

Vic took a deep breath as he rubbed his temples. "Okay, we need to talk about this."

"Talk about what? We didn't talk about it last time," I said casually, taking another sip of my drink.

Vic's eyes went wide. "What do you mean 'last time'?"

"Vic, you can't be serious. The last time we had sex!"

"Are you serious?" Vic held his head between his hands. "That's why I woke up in the back lounge!"

"Yeah..."

Turns out, Vic blacked out that first night. All he remembered was taking shots and then waking up in an empty back lounge when the bus arrived at the hotel in DC.

"Why didn't you say anything?" he asked.

"When you acted completely normal, I figured we weren't gonna talk about it. Just move on like nothing happened."

"Ugh. Wait, did we use a condom?!"

"Honestly, I can't remember. I was pretty drunk too. But I took a Plan B the next morning."

He relaxed into his seat and sat back, looking into the night sky. "Well, that was smart of you."

"Yeah..." I was unsure how to reply to that.

For the next fifteen minutes, he paced the balcony, staring at the ocean. Then he sat down with his head buried in his hands again. "How could I do this? I've never cheated before. What am I supposed to do now? I messed up bad."

I sat silently. He seemed to be experiencing all the emotions I had after the first time we'd slept together. Only I didn't have a fiancée to answer to.

He broke the stillness with a question. "Did you cum the first time?"

"No, but it's okay. I rarely came with my ex. I think it only happens for me with women."

A hint of a smile formed in the corner of his lips. He got up, stood in front of my chair, and held out his hand. "Well, I'm willing to prove you wrong."

I took his hand and followed him into my hotel room. This time, I knew *exactly* how the hell I got here.

31
eating me alive

I wish I could blame mixing alcohol for my sexcapades with Vic. But unfortunately alcohol was not to blame, 'cause during the following week, we repeated these events multiple times, most of which I was stone-cold sober for. After shows. In an empty dressing room. On the empty tour bus in the back lounge or in his bunk. In my hotel room or his. And every time, he would ask the infamous question: "Did you cum?"

I felt so embarrassed. So ashamed. I started to lie. I thought something was wrong with me. There had to be a way I could make it happen. So every time the energy stirred, I tried different techniques to get to my climax. The last time we had sex, I got on top, and for some reason the stars aligned—or maybe it was the slight curve of his appendage—and I reached my climax. It was the first time he said "You came" instead of asking if I had. Once he'd finished, I went back to my hotel room and everything changed.

I stayed up thinking for hours. Not about my victory, that I'd climaxed with a man. I didn't think about how many times we'd done the deed before that moment. I didn't daydream about doing it again. The only thought on my mind, the only thing plaguing my brain, was his fiancée.

"How could I do this?!" I yelled to my friend Crystal on the phone. "Like, how did I end up here?! I prefer women. I've preferred women for most of my dating life. How could I be out here smashing a man with a fiancée?! I'm out here dogging this woman. How could I do that to another woman when I love women?!"

Crystal consoled me the best she could.

When I recounted the events to SHE months later, she laughed in my face.

"You started thinking about all of that after you came? Then reality hit you? You had post-nut clarity!" she said.

"Yesssssss," I said between giggles. "I guess I did have PNC!"

In the spirit of PNC, I texted Vic the next morning.

ME

Hey, can I come to your room? I wanna talk to you about something.

VIC

Yeah.

In a long, one-breath, run-on sentence, I told Vic about my feelings. The guilt I felt because I was hurting another woman.

The internal chaos I felt because I was doing things with a man at a time when men weren't really on my radar. My fear of making the rest of the tour awkward for us. My emotions spewed all over that hotel room.

When I'd finished speaking, silence fell. He stared down at his lap for what felt like an eternity. Then he finally said, "This has been eating me alive."

Relief trickled down my shoulders as I audibly exhaled.

"Really? 'Cause on the outside, you seem to be doing all of this with ease."

"Yeah, on the outside. But on the inside, what I've been doing to my fiancée has been keeping me up at night."

This snowballed into a three-hour conversation about anything and everything: Our overwhelming guilt. How to stop whatever this was from developing any further. My limited experience with men. The circus that was tour, hormones, and alcohol. At the end of the conversation, we agreed that this thing would end immediately.

Though I was curious, I never asked if he planned on telling his fiancée. Whatever he decided to do from here on out was none of my business, so I had no place to ask. When it came to me, however, Vic had all the questions.

"So you getting back with your ex-boyfriend?"

"Ha! Never."

"You gonna start talking to women again?"

"Shoot, most likely. But I need some time alone before any of that."

He looked confused. His gaze wandered out the window like

he was searching for the perfect way to ask his next question. After a few long seconds, he turned to me and spit it out. "Are you gonna start dating Sheopatra?"

Huh?!

My neck retracted backward instantly. Why would he bring her name up? She and I were in the same dance collective. She was one of my friends. Someone I loved spending time with, who made me laugh a lot and just so happened to be stunning, but all those feelings were internal. At least, I thought they were.

"Um... To be honest, I have no idea what's gonna happen there."

After the initial shock of Vic acknowledging some unspoken energy between SHE and me, my next thought was, *It's none of his damn business.*

Despite Vic's slight investigation into my life after him, I felt so content with our conversation. No, not content—I was absolutely *floored*. I thought it had been a real, sane adult conversation. A mutual agreement to continue a professional relationship and keep sex out of it. A surefire way for us to finish out the last three months of the tour unscathed. To my nineteen-year-old brain, I was a boss-ass bitch. I'd put my big-girl panties on and gotten down to business.

"Whew, I'm so glad we had this talk," I said. "Now we can finish out this job without any mess and keep it moving."

"Yeah, I'm glad we had this talk too. This thing between us has really been bothering me."

I slung my purse over my shoulder and walked toward the

door. "Well, now we can both be at peace, and you can focus on your relationship."

Silence filled the air once again. I reached out to turn the doorknob, but something stopped me dead in my tracks. Something saying, "Don't leave. Stay." The feeling was strong, making the air feel as thick as a humid morning. And the feeling sure as hell didn't come from me.

As a matter of fact, it wasn't a *feeling* at all. It wasn't an air or an atmosphere. It was a hundred percent physical, 'cause it was Vic embracing me from behind, his full-blown erection poking at my back.

A week before, this probably would've made me buckle. What kind of spicy romance-novel scene was this?! Girl tries to leave the room but falls into another passionate scene of love-making (though I wouldn't describe what we had done as *making love*). Before I visited his room to talk, this would've sent my pants straight to my ankles.

But now, I felt different. This wasn't sexy. It wasn't a movie scene. It was a waste of my time!

Three hours.

Three hours of hearing this man talk about how this thing was "eating him alive," that he'd never cheated before. The drama, 180 minutes of fake guilt and reconciliation, just to get up, hug me from behind, and act like nothing happened. None of the words I'd said were important? None of my wishes mattered?!

Smoke poured from my ears. With everything in me, I

wanted to turn around and call him all kinds of profanities, tell him he ain't shit and his fiancée needs to move on.

But I simply inhaled, exhaled, and said, "No." Then I walked out of his room.

32
a break

This cat-and-mouse game continued for the next two months. By this point my system was a well-oiled "no" machine. Over time, he became less persistent, but I still had to make sure we didn't end up alone together. Nothing could save me from the stage, though.

For this tour, Vic and I had a contemporary duet about a couple with intense physical energy. In the dance, the couple finally succumbed to their feelings for one another. The choreography was filled with close-contact partnering, lifts, and moments of love.

While we were sleeping together, that duet was the highlight of every show. I pushed the limits every time, prolonging touches for as long as I could, letting our bodies perform the lifts as one. I even glanced down at his crotch from time to time to see if his off-stage desire peeked through on stage. Everything had a sexual undertone to it—an undertone I swore was only detectable by the two of us. But during one show, I heard an audience member gasp over the music. The tension was palpable. It was a wild week.

When our tourmance ended, the duet transformed. He brought his cat-and-mouse game to the stage. He'd slide his hands beneath my waistline during lifts. Deliver piercing eye contact that was beyond acting. Whisper things in my ear I can't even include in this book. During those two minutes and forty seconds, he took full advantage of the personal barriers that routine broke.

Between that wild week and the weeks following our sizzling tourmance, my performance changed very little. I no longer prolonged touch or stretched out the close moments, but I did get the story across: friends to lovers, angst, and infatuation. My performance showcased all the sensuality in the world, which I then switched off as soon as I stepped into the wings and the last seconds of the song faded away.

I knew my acting skills were pristine because Vic brought them up during his late-night cat-and-mouse games.

"I see the way you look at me on stage. I know you want this too."

If I'm being honest, my hormones wanted it, but my brain and heart couldn't withstand the consequences. I'm thankful the consequences outweighed my hormones every time.

Around this time in the tour, Rosa spent most of her off time with Leo. She only came around when her ever-growing feelings for him became too much. I'm not sure how Vic spent his off time; I tried to avoid him like the plague.

I spent most of my free time before shows, after shows, and on off days with the rest of the male dancers. Whenever the bus call wasn't seconds after the show, we'd find ourselves raging in the LGBTQ+ parts of the city. I was the only girl in the bunch, so the odds of us ending up in a lesbian club were slim, but some nights I got lucky and there'd be a random girl among a large group of gay men just like me. She'd walk in and we might exchange looks, but that would be the end of it. I didn't gain the courage to go further until a random phone conversation with Sheopatra.

For the first time since the tour started, we spoke on the phone. Because of the fresh embarrassment in the pit of my stomach, I decided not to tell her about Vic. That wouldn't happen until later. But during that call, I did disclose my newfound nightlife.

"Oh, gay clubs in different cities? That sounds like so much fun. Get some numbers!" SHE replied.

"Ha! Numbers?! I wish. I saw this pretty girl at the club we were at last night, but I couldn't speak."

"What?! Naw. Next time, just go up to her and start a conversation about anything. Get that number or Instagram handle!"

(To this day, I still can't believe the friend who encouraged me to get numbers at the club is now my wife.)

That phone conversation gifted me with a different mojo the next time we went out. A few minutes after entering a club in another random city, I laid eyes on a gorgeous mocha-toned girl with an Afro. She had on long gold earrings and dark-brown lip gloss. Jean shorts hugged her hips and thighs like magic.

As soon as the next song rang through the speakers, I made my way over and started dancing with her, our hips swaying to the music. The glitter around her eyes sparkled in the club lights. Never missing a beat, she grabbed my hands and pulled me closer. I let my hands rest on her waist. When the song ended, she didn't seem to have any intention of leaving, so I let my hands drop to her thighs. Her soft-as-cocoa-butter legs sent waves through my entire body.

The group of coworkers I'd arrived with—mostly male dancers and a few female dancers—were two-stepping in the VIP section. No matter how hard they tried to conceal it, I could see their stunned faces from a mile away. Loads of questions were probably circling their brains, but I didn't care. I kept my focus on the beautiful mocha girl in front of me. This was a needed break from the pitiful cat-and-mouse game I'd been forced to play. This time, there was no unwanted chase. The feelings were mutual.

At the end of the night, we started walking back to the bus. Because of our varying degrees of alcohol intake, all six dancers moved at different paces. Some spoke loudly. Others used the streets as their backdrop and kept dancing as we traveled. I think one of the dancers vomited in a bush, but I can't be sure; my attention was on the beautiful mocha girl with an Afro walking me back to the bus. By this time, I'd learned her name was Keonna.

She planned to call her Uber from our bus since it wasn't too far from the club. But when we arrived at the bus with twenty minutes to spare before departure, we kept talking while the rest of the crew trickled onboard. I didn't want to leave. I didn't want to snap back to reality. I didn't want to wonder if Vic was still awake and waiting to play cat and mouse. I just wanted to spend these last few moments with Keonna.

When her Uber pulled up, we exchanged numbers, followed each other on social media, and hugged goodbye. Before fully releasing me, she glided her index finger from the base of my neck to my chin. With gentle pressure, she turned my chin to the right and landed a soft, slow kiss on my left cheek, just centimeters away from my lips. Then she brought her hand back down to mine and said, "Have a great night. It was so nice meeting you."

As I boarded the bus, my cheek buzzed.

Deep down, I knew I would never see her again, but I was so thankful for this night. A much-needed break from the chaos of this tour. A night off from strategizing about how I'd deal with Vic. For a few moments, I could just breathe and live my life.

And most of all, I loved how Keonna didn't push. When she kissed me on the cheek, she didn't go for my mouth. Her hands never roamed my body. The most she did was graze her fingers along my chin and down my arm. It was a breath of fresh air, a walk in the park on a sunny day, compared to the games Vic had been playing these past few weeks.

When I boarded the bus, some of my coworkers gave me knowing glances.

The rest of the cast either acted like they hadn't seen, or like they did but were no longer surprised. While one person brushed her teeth, another organized his shoes, and someone else talked about the messy cabinets, Vic stood in the middle of the bus completely still, his eyes locked on mine.

I paused for a second, wondering if he'd seen Keonna and me. And if he had seen, why the hell did he have that hurt look on his face? Why couldn't he just...?

Then I hushed the thoughts, every one of them. I looked down and walked straight past him. I had a good-ass time, finally, and there was no way he was about to ruin it.

About a month later, I'd find myself in the same position, outside the bus late at night seeing another woman off. But this time, it would be Sheopatra. And instead of a kiss on the cheek, we'd be in a full-blown make-out session. But by that time, I didn't care about anybody's reactions, not my coworkers, or Vic's.

33
meet and greet

Have you ever felt like someone was staring at you, even though you couldn't spot them? That undeniable, almost instinctual feeling that someone was looking at you? *That's* what I felt. But instead of being in a big space, unsure of who was staring at me, I was at a meet and greet inside a small theater lobby with my castmates' eyes surveying my every move. Even the artist peered over at me a couple of times. Why? Because somehow, out of all the cities in the country, Vic's fiancée had decided to attend *this* meet and greet in a random city in Idaho.

Her gorgeous brown face floated among a crowd of mostly white faces. Never more than a foot away from her future husband, she admired each interaction he shared with the fans, delighted to get to experience this world with her other half. On the opposite end of the room, I was in my own world—full of tension, discomfort, and more discomfort. While I absently mingled with fans, I tried to hold on like a mobile home in a twister. I smiled, signed autographs, and engaged in as much small talk as possible.

"Hey there!" someone said, tapping me from behind.

I spun around. My eyes locked with hers and then fell to her outfit. A brown head wrap held her curls while a few tendrils fell to the sides. A long, oversized cardigan draped her frame, from her shoulders to her ankles. And then there was the last detail: Birkenstock sandals, footwear I jokingly called "Jesus 11s." But it wasn't so funny now that *she* had them on. From the headwrap and cardigan down to the Jesus 11s, we were dressed identically. . What kind of *Punk'd*, *Sister Wives*, and *Cheaters* mash-up episode had I walked into?! My mobile home couldn't withstand any more, and I got pulled up into the funnel.

"Oh, hey! How are you?" I ignored the sweat pooling in my armpits.

Light shone from her eyes. "I'm well! I'm so excited to see the show tonight. Your duet with Vic has so many likes and comments online. I can't wait to see it in person."

If only she knew about the dance we used to perform off stage, I thought.

"Oh, really? I hadn't noticed. My Instagram's been acting up lately."

She smiled and looked at the group of little girls patiently waiting behind me. "Anyways, I'll let you get to it. Good luck tonight!"

I turned to the group of girls, all dressed in their studio's merchandise: bright-pink shirts that said "Rising Star Dance Company." They might as well have worn red capes around their necks considering how they saved me.

While I interacted with this group, my mind spiraled. The freeness with which his fiancée had spoken to me could only mean two things:

1. She didn't know a thing about Vic and me. Or...

2. She knew and was trying to throw me off. Maybe she saw me sweating. Maybe she got off on my discomfort.

The second option was possible, but there was just no way. Her smile was too genuine. Her sweet demeanor was undeniable.

I'd just had small talk with Vic's beautiful, unsuspecting future wife, and everything came to a head. That feeling of being the "other woman"—not from afar, but right there in real time. Embarrassment because all my coworkers knew. In between all their pictures, thank you's, and autographs, they were stealing glances in my direction to watch the soap-opera scene unfold before them. That we were dressed like we'd gone shopping together the day before. Then there was the overflow of shame pouring into the pit of my stomach.

I can't even begin to describe how the show went that night because it's all a blur. My body performed the steps just like every other night, but my mind was a tornado.

How the hell did I get here?

34

the next job

Piece by piece, I packed my carry-on bag with undergarments and toiletries, twirling around my room to the sounds of Earth, Wind & Fire. After tossing a pair of shoes into my bag, I paused to perform some vocals to the invisible audience on my bed. After a two-week break in LA, a reset I'd desperately needed, I was preparing to fly to San Francisco for the last show on the HDIGH Tour.

Though I hadn't even gotten to the airport yet, I already felt like I'd finished the job and made it through some of the toughest months of my life. One of the hardest jobs of my career. I could practically taste the heavy breaths leaving my lungs as we performed our final bow. I fantasized about returning to the airport the morning after the show and flying back to LA, eager to audition for my next job, *any* job, far away from Vic and his cat-and-mouse game. I was so ready to close this chapter of my life that I refused to pack an actual suitcase. A carry-on would do just fine; I only needed the essentials for my final moments on this roller coaster ride. The end was near. While most of the cast shared emotional goodbyes, I braced myself for the future ahead.

Everyone handled the last show differently. Some people's sadness looked like visible dark clouds over their heads. Some weren't ready for their dream job to come to an end. Others weren't ready to be thrown back into the world of freelancing. One of the male dancers purchased a disposable camera and photographed every moment of the last show. From the theater lobby to the catering provided in the dining hall, he'd have evidence of it all. A couple of people, myself included, simply wondered, *What's next?*

Even our tour manager had a different air. Her blonde hair laid down her back in soft waves instead of the tight French twist she'd rocked all tour. Uber reimbursements and per diem for our last show day seemed to be the only tasks left on her list. After that, our problems were no longer her concern. Her aura screamed teacher on the last day of school: "Behave, watch this random movie, and try to keep it together until the bell rings." The crew guys set up the stage and then hung around the back of the theater like it was a tailgate party, playing cards, drinking beer, and listening to music. Rosa wore a somber expression for most of the day, but not because it was the end of a dream job or a consistent income; her biggest worry was the fate of her romance with Leo. In the last months of tour, they'd become an unofficial–official item, and she wasn't ready to return to their respective cities.

I, on the other hand, was a ray of sunshine. With a permanent smile glued to my face, I floated through breakfast catering, the dressing room, and the theater lobby. With five hours to showtime, I decided to clean out my bunk on the bus. There wasn't much left outside of my chargers, memory-foam pillow, and fuzzy blanket, but it was best to clean it out now; there was no telling how I'd feel after the show. Excitement might hit me so hard that I'd fly all the way back to LA and forget there was ever a bunk to clean.

But after taking two steps onto the bus, those sunshine rays came to a halt. Vic was sitting in the front lounge of the bus in silence.

Desperate to make this moment any less awkward, I forced small talk. "Hey."

"Hey."

"Uh, how was your two-week break? Feel rested?"

He buried his forehead into the palm of his right hand. "Not that good. I decided to come clean and tell my fiancée about us."

I couldn't help but think, *Us? What does he mean by us?* I was glad he'd finally told her the truth, but I prayed he didn't actually think there was an *us*.

"How did she take it?" A dumb question, but I had no clue what else to say.

"She lost it. Threatened to break off the engagement, move out, everything."

"I'm so sorry," I forced myself to say. Inside, I silently rooted for his fiancée to end things. She deserved so much more.

"Yeah, I think we need to keep space between us."

I fell silent. Dumbfounded. Peeved beyond belief. How did he have the *audacity* to introduce this idea of "space" as if it were something new? As if that hadn't been my goal during these last months of tour? A goal he threatened every time he had a few drinks?

Despite the feelings stirring within me, I bit my tongue. "Okay, yeah. I totally understand."

The conversation ended as quickly as it had begun. As my feelings faded, I decided not to let Vic taint my last tour show. I would gladly give him space if it prevented this show from being stressful. I cleaned my bunk and then went to the female dressing room to do my makeup, completely unaware of what was in store for me.

It wasn't just his disconnected eye contact; I'd grown accustomed to his wavering presence during our onstage partnering. Some shows, his eyes wandered the room, looking at anything but me. Other shows, his desire reignited, and his gaze penetrated mine. And during a few shows, I could tell he was doing everything in his power to keep it professional.

This night was different.

Because of the news he'd recently told his fiancée, I assumed this show would be a disconnected one, or perhaps professional. Boy, was I wrong. During our duet, everything—from minor choreographed touches, to important lifts and tricks, down to his gaze—was filled with distaste, repulsion, and something that felt a lot like anger. I'd never experienced this side of him before, and I hated it.

My thoughts turned cold. How *dare* he sabotage the last show of this tour! I'd been doing my job on and off stage for months. I hadn't fully let loose after the shows because I had to track his whereabouts and alcohol intake. I was patient with that dreadful cat-and-mouse game because I was young and figured that's what men do when you cross that boundary.

How *dare* he look at me like I was the demise of his relationship! I mean, I most definitely was, but it takes two to have sex, and I was the one who called it off. I was the one who resisted every advance he made for months. And if it weren't for me, he and I would've had sex for the entire tour instead of just one week.

This was the last straw. All my patience had dried up.

After the show, I showered, wiped off my makeup, had one glass of wine with my castmates, and went to sleep. But in my dreams I was already in LA on the next job or audition, far away from Vic and the rest of the tour.

———

Two weeks after that last show, I was working a new job, having just inhaled the sandwich on my plate. "Whew! I'm so glad they called lunch early. I swear my breakfast evaporated from my stomach!"

Sabrina, one of the women I'd become close to on this awards show job, clutched her stomach while giggles spilled over. "Yours? My stomach was growling LOUD. I could've sworn the choreographer heard it!"

"Those problems belong to the past, 'cause this food here never had a chance." I performed my best chef's kiss to celebrate the Jersey Mike's sub that had saved my life, causing us both to giggle more.

"Girl, you crazy. All this laughing got my face hurting... Hey." She paused, her laughter coming to a halt. "Can I ask you a question?"

"Uh, yeah. Sure."

"Are you and Vic not cool with each other? I can't help but notice how much y'all stay clear of one another. Every day you come to rehearsal, say hi, hug everyone, and skip over him. He does the same. I thought y'all would be close friends 'cause of that tour y'all were just on..."

I wanted to finish her sentence so badly. We *would* be close friends if I hadn't had sex with him and helped eventually implode his engagement. After a roller coaster of a tour, the last thing I wanted was to be in the same room as Vic. Then God said, "Hey! You're going to do your first after-tour job with Vic."

"Damn... Is it that obvious?"

And just like that, the laughter returned, lightening the air.

"Uh, yeah! You two live on separate sides of the studio all day."

"Ugh, we're cool. We just aren't on speaking terms. We keep it cordial. A lot happens in four months. People crave space, they miss home. Some people are morning people, others aren't. Everyone has different lifestyles, then you slap them on a bus together. We just need space. Maybe things will change down the road."

"Four months? Oh, Lord, I would lose my mind! I can't imagine being away from my boyfriend for that long."

"Oh, Facetime would become your best friend." I laughed it off, praying Sabrina hadn't sensed my discomfort and thankful she hadn't pushed for more information.

That job changed everything: my interactions, my intentions, my focus. Though it was a wild ride, I'm grateful for the lessons. For someone as hardheaded as myself, the lessons had to be dramatic for them to stick.

While I'm sure you took your own tips and tricks from my story, here's one more pro tip: No matter how tempting it might be, try not to sleep with *anyone* on tour. Most tourmances aren't the shit show mine was, but they do tend to fizzle out once the job is over. Tours place you in a bubble: the same people, close spaces, different temperaments. I've witnessed a tourmance bud because two dancers were the only explorers in the group. While most of us used our off time to rest, eat, and shop, they went snorkeling and skydiving, or did whatever other adventures the city had to offer. It took no time for deeper feelings to kick in. When the tour ended, however, they quickly realized they didn't have much else in common.

If you feel those palpitating heartbeats on tour, try to hold on to your wits until the end of the job. After both of you return to LA, go on dates and get to know one another in "normal life."

35

episode three

Welcome to episode three of "Yoe Gets Fired from a Job."

This one didn't hurt a bit. I didn't feel betrayed by a black choreographer. God didn't graciously save me from a job I didn't have the courage to leave. This time, I bowed out peacefully. My spirit said, "Hell no!" while my mouth politely said, "No, thank you. Y'all can go on without me."

The beginning of the pandemic was an interesting time. The entertainment industry was at a standstill for weeks. Production companies either couldn't film at all or were forced to figure out ways to do so with a third of their workers.

Many brands relied on influencers to continue marketing. I get influencer work here and there, though I'm extremely picky about the brands I choose to represent. I'd rather my social platforms remain a place for my art and passions. I push for Yoe the

Brand instead of the newest weight-loss tea. However, when the pandemic hit, brand work came pouring in. Companies quickly noticed that my home served as its own mini production studio. My wife was the videographer, editor, set designer, and talent, and I assisted her however I needed to. By the grace of God, we stayed afloat during these tough times because of this unforeseen work.

Toward the end of the year I received an Instagram message from a choreographer named Amber.

> **AMBER**
>
> Hey! Hope all is well. I'm working on a performance with an R&B artist, and I would love to have you be a part. Who's your agent?

A few days and emails later, I was attending rehearsal for an hour-long show. It was a learning curve to return to dance work outside of my home studio. Even though we had to dance with masks on and arrive an hour early to take rapid tests every morning, I was excited to leave my house for something other than grocery store trips. I'd been ready for a glimpse into this post-pandemic world.

After a couple of days of rehearsal, Amber got comfortable. "Since we're testing every day, I don't mind if y'all take your masks off once you're cleared."

From that moment on, we continued with our regularly scheduled programming. We'd arrive at rehearsal by 9 a.m., get swabbed, and wait outside until the results rolled in. Testing added more time to our already long day, but I didn't mind. I spent the hour sunbathing outside my car in an outdoor folding chair—a nice change from the fluorescent lights and black walls in the dance studio.

One morning, while I was soaking up some vitamin D, the COVID tester appeared in front of me. "You have to retake the test."

My armpits immediately started sweating. As he swabbed more thoroughly, I asked, "Did my test come back positive?"

As calm as a day-spa attendant, he said, "Yes, we're retesting you as a precaution. Don't worry. False positives happen all the time."

My mind became loud and chaotic as I sat back in my folding chair, trying to be cool and collected. I watched as the rest of the dancers were cleared to enter the studio. With each cleared dancer, my anxiety worsened. Eventually I was the only person left outside.

Fifteen minutes later, the tester returned. "It came back negative. You can go inside."

"Really?! Whew, you had me sweating for a second!" I smiled from ear to ear as I grabbed my belongings.

Then I overheard the tester on the phone with Amber. "Yeah, Christine's results just came back. She's good to go."

"Wait..." I started.

Then I heard Amber through the phone. "Wait, what do you mean? Christine is right next to me. You have Yoe out there."

It only took fifteen minutes. Fifteen minutes of maskless stretching inside the dance studio, and over the next week, we dropped like flies. A new person tested positive each day, four dancers in total, all because they'd mixed up Christine and me. Four days later, my time had come. I tested positive and they sent me home, where I quarantined in our guest bedroom.

Every morning, I turned over and sniffed a bottle of peppermint oil as hard as my lungs would allow, just to make sure my sense of smell was still intact. Thankfully, I never lost it, but I did suffer from extreme fatigue. It was as if I had narcolepsy. No matter what I did, grogginess took over. I fell asleep while eating meals and took two whole days to finish one episode of a show. One night I slept for fourteen hours. After a couple of days, the fatigue subsided, and I patiently waited out the rest of my quarantine.

The hours I spent in that bedroom left me with plenty of time to think, and I realized something. I'd been so excited about my first dance job during the pandemic that I wasn't even sure what exactly the performance was for. It couldn't have been for a live performance since COVID restrictions prevented audiences from entering arenas and stadiums. Only one possibility remained: the job was being streamed.

After a quick round of emails to my agent, my suspicions were confirmed. The show would be streamed and sponsored by a Big Tech company, but with that clarity came bad news. The artist's camp only planned to pay for the show with no buyout. No compensation for our faces, and our bodies, being broadcasted to thousands of viewers. In the past, a lack of buyout— and a lack of appropriate contractual language—had allowed a camp to use footage of me for social media marketing and a documentary. They continued to make a profit while I received nothing.

It's more common for camps to offer low-grade buyouts, but to offer nothing at all is blasphemous. I requested that my agent fight for the buyout even if they agreed to a lower number than I anticipated. No matter what, I didn't want a camp as established as this one to get used to disrespecting dancers. I was prepared to negotiate for the remaining days of my quarantine. Unfortunately, the negotiation ended a couple of hours later when I received an email from my agent.

Subject: Buyout

Hey there,

Regarding the buyout, the camp is not going to budge. They have asked me to inform you that the offer stays as is. You may take it or be released from the job.

I responded immediately.

Re: Buyout

Tell them to release me.

Minutes after hitting send, my phone rang. "Hey, Yoe! It's Amber."

"Hey, love! How are you?"

"I'm good. Hey, before we move forward, I just wanna ask... Are you sure?"

"Oh, yes. I am most definitely sure. It's customary to be paid a buyout for something like this, even if it's a low one. The fact that the camp wasn't even willing to negotiate a lower buyout says a lot. I don't want to accept this. I don't want them to think this kind of treatment is okay."

"I understand. But when it comes to this industry and longevity in a camp, certain sacrifices have to be made. Tour rehearsals are starting in a couple of months. Think about it. You lose a little bit now to make fifty thousand later on tour."

I paused, considering the real response I wanted to give her: *Thank you for the lesson, but it's also important to build relationships off integrity and respect. Otherwise this fight never ends; it'll just fade out and resurface later. If I say yes to this, what's to stop them from doing the same thing when the tour footage airs? Furthermore, the tour is yearlong. I've made fifty thousand with one commercial over the span of three months. Lastly, how about respecting an artist's decision next time instead of trying to convince them otherwise?*

I inhaled those words and exhaled the only thing I could say politely. "I understand, but no, thank you."

"Okay, well, I tried. I'm sorry things had to end like this."

Amber's words forced a chuckle from my throat. "End like what? I can promise you, I actually like y'all's camp. That's rare for me! Everyone was chill, productive, sweet—it was great. I saw you even brought alternates in to learn our tracks while some of us were out with COVID. That made my decision to leave so much easier. I can't tell you how many times I've wanted to walk off a job, but my heart felt for the dancers and choreographers scrambling to teach a new dancer or change formations. I've been on that end before and it wasn't fun. I feel a thousand percent better knowing there's already a dancer in my spot. It's less work and stress on you guys."

Perhaps my response threw Amber off, 'cause she got off the phone at the speed of light. Had she expected me to be upset? Did she think she'd convince me by mentioning fifty thousand dollars? I didn't know, but it was no longer my concern.

I later learned that the young woman who'd taken my spot was originally from another country and had been living in the US on a work visa. When the pandemic caused the industry to come to a standstill, she didn't find work for months and was ineligible for aid. And because her work visa was specifically for dance, she wasn't legally allowed to seek any other kind of work in the meantime. Amber bringing her in to fill my spot may have kept her from having to return to her home country. My heart felt full knowing that, in some strange way, I'd helped her.

The fight for a buyout was a lonely one. Out of twelve dancers, I was the only one to push back, but I didn't mind. Even outside of a pandemic, dance work can be perpetually unstable. I'm in no position to look into people's pockets and coerce them into threatening their jobs (though it probably would've been more effective to fight back as a group). Amber's phone call carried the slightest condescension, but that didn't bother me much either. What peeved me the most was the tour manager's behavior.

At the end of the next day, Max, a male dancer in the camp, texted me.

MAX

Question, are you coming back?
Someone else has been holding your
spot since you've been gone, but today
Amber gave it to her permanently.

ME

No, I won't be coming back. I couldn't
agree to do a show with an established
artist, sponsored by a tech company,
with no buyout. I didn't tell anyone
because I didn't want to pressure
people.

MAX

Really??? Wow, that makes so much
sense now. The tour manager gave us
such a weird lecture today.

ME

A lecture? What did he say?

MAX

He busted through the doors in the
middle of a break, pink in the face,
yelling, "We do so much for you all! We
take good care of you guys! I'm not
saying you should be grateful, but
there's worse treatment out there!"

ME

Lol. So basically, "I'm not saying you
should be grateful, but you should be
grateful!"

MAX

Right. I was confused until I overheard him and Amber talking about how you weren't accepting the buyout. Or nonexistent buyout lol.

Though I hadn't been present for the tour manager's outburst, it boiled my blood. His actions were uncalled for and unprofessional.

I'd made my decision rather quickly. I requested a buyout once, and they declined it. There wasn't a long drawn-out negotiation process. I didn't inform the other dancers of my decision. I didn't rally the troops and attempt to go on strike. Most of them were unaware of what had happened. So why was he mad? There was absolutely no reason for his tantrum. It seemed like one big, ugly display of power to me. A reminder to the rest of the cast to stay in their places and not ask for more.

It took me a few years to learn this, but whether you're let go from or choose to leave a job, you will be fine. It won't define your entire career. And don't be afraid to say no. It's one of the most empowering things I've ever learned how to do.

36

amor

I don't know what it was exactly. No matter where we were in our relationship, SHE displayed never-ending patience for me. The entire ordeal with Vic left me wishing for peace, and I wanted time alone to get reacquainted with myself. When I wasn't ready to hop into a relationship right away, SHE waited for me. She didn't pressure me into a union or move on to the next.

Was it that her family stressed the importance of loving one another and being there for people, cultivating her beautiful personality? Was it the God-given talent that seeped from her pores, not only in dance but in other avenues as well? Or was it those captivating hazel eyes that changed colors on certain days?

I don't know when I started falling for Sheopatra. I don't think there was one tidal wave of feelings, just gentle reminders over time—God constantly nudging me, saying, "Hold on to her." The kind of reminders I used to think were meant for platonic relationships.

Her southern charm made me feel like I wasn't too far from home. She pushed me to improve my craft. Ever since I touched down in LA, she welcomed me with open arms. "Keep her in your life," my intuition told me. This unmistakable knowing later transformed into questions: Why did my stomach flutter when I saw her? Why did I miss her when she was gone? And the most troubling question—how dare she be that beautiful?

The day I met SHE at an audition, I had no clue I was staring at my future wife.

My dating history pre-Sheopatra was a wildfire. She dropped into my life during a time I would describe as the Dark Ages. I was like a fork rattling around in a garbage disposal, and our friendship was everything I needed. She poured life into me, the scared young woman who had just moved to a new city. She encouraged me and helped me believe in my gifts. And somewhere along the way, things evolved.

A few days after breaking up with my boyfriend, I asked SHE to hang out after rehearsal. I was newly single, about to go on a four-month tour, and in the process of avoiding my best friend, Karina. I was spiraling. I craved guidance and an outside perspective on the situation.

I finished rehearsal at 7 p.m., grabbed some food with her at 8 p.m., and when it was time for her to drop me off at the hotel at around 10 p.m., we talked in her car until three in the morning—beginning the after-rehearsal pattern that would continue till the day I left.

Sheopatra effortlessly distracted me from my life. We'd session, create content, eat good food, and laugh until we cried. Compared to everything else going on in my life, hanging with her was a necessary change of pace. I didn't mind losing a little sleep over it, which is why I'd leave her car at 6 a.m. some nights. For the last week and a half of rehearsals, I spent every evening with SHE, all of it feeling strictly platonic—until my last night in LA.

That day, rehearsal went smoothly. Because we'd been working hard for weeks, the choreographer decided to take it easy on us. After running the show twice, they released us early, allowing me ample time to shower, pack up my hotel room, and spend more time with SHE on my last day in town.

After devouring some wings, we drove to a gorgeous walking trail at the base of a mountain. She set up her camera equipment, and we shot multiple videos with the greenery as our background. (Though I'm an entirely different dancer now, watching these videos still brings a smile to my face.) At around 10 p.m., we pulled up to my hotel to continue the same routine we'd been following the past week. She offered to cut our conversation short, insisting I should get rest for my travel day tomorrow, but each time I refused. I was determined to spend every last minute with her. (Nothing gets between me and my sleep. I should've known then that she was the one!)

We talked about celebrities, dance culture, and high school memories. At around 2 a.m., we fell into a conversation about hair textures.

"I remember the first time I saw someone go natural," SHE

said. "This girl I went to ballet school with had left the program. She had chemically straightened hair. When she came back a year later, her hair was curly and down to her shoulders. I was blown away! I immediately asked how she got her hair like that, and she said, 'I went natural.'"

"I feel you," I said. "I didn't even know my hair was curly! The first time someone curled my hair instead of putting it in a style or straightening it, I thought the mousse was the magic that blessed me with curls. I didn't know the product was just accentuating what I already had."

We shared laughs.

"I've never really been close to somebody with your texture before. Can I touch it?" SHE asked.

"Yeah, go ahead!"

She reached out, resting the palm of her hand at the base of my neck, then stretched her fingers into my hair. Feeling, scratching, exploring. Head rubs usually make me lethargic, but this time, another feeling crept in.

The once-cool car became warmer. The sounds on the radio drifted away. My breathing slowed slightly. The longer SHE's fingers were in my hair, the higher my temperature rose. We were friends; I'd never felt this way any other time we'd touched. But something about this touch was personal, intimate, and I never wanted it to end. I craved nothing more than for her to touch more parts of me. That's when I knew I was no longer her friend.

I wanted more than that.

I planned to keep in contact with her on tour through text

and Facetime, giving myself time to see how these budding feelings would evolve. That was the plan, until I slept with Vic on the tour. By then I was dealing with a tornado of problems, and I felt like I couldn't pursue SHE after that fiasco. She was a beautiful human being, inside and out. Someone who deserved the world, not a messy girl who'd fallen into a tourmance in the blink of an eye. So I avoided her calls and texts.

Toward the end of the tour, I missed her energy so much that I began to let her in a little. I told her about the cities I'd visited and the clubs we'd partied at, but I completely left out the intel on Vic and me.

Even hundreds of miles away, SHE knew something was off. "Hey, I know we had a bit of energy before you left. But I wanna let you know you aren't mine. Don't get me wrong, I have feelings for you, but we aren't together. Don't feel like you can't live your life on tour. Something tells me you already have... And if you have, that's okay. Take your time. Explore. I'll wait for you."

Silence draped between us. I thanked God we weren't on Facetime so she didn't have to witness my absent expression, matching my lack of words. I inhaled and then word-vomited into the phone, speed-talking through the roller coaster ride of my tourmance. I probably talked in circles, jumbling all my thoughts together. And after what felt like a five-minute monologue, I finished speaking. I pressed the phone harder into my ear, desperate for a rebuttal, a breath, a word—anything.

After what felt like an eternity, SHE chuckled and began her response, "Thanks for telling me..."

I've been off the market for quite some time, but from what I can see through the lens of those around me, dating in Los Angeles is still wild. It's a highly flammable material ready to flare up at any moment.

On the plus side, this is a huge city populated with all kinds of people. In the City of Angels, the odds are high you'll find a relationship that fits your needs. Gay, straight, no gender roles in the home, strict gender roles in the home, poly, trans, rock-climbing duos, festival lovebirds—the possibilities are endless.

We all have layers, and it's up to us to reveal them to our partners. Every transplant who chose to move here has a story. Almost every native has enough stories to make up a novel. Dating is such a specific experience, with specific personalities, in specific moments of your life. Because it's so personal to each person's experience, I don't like to give a lot of advice on the topic, but here are a few tips that have worked for me:

- No matter how angry you are at your partner, don't call them out of their name.
- If you're in a serial dating or sexually liberal stage, consider the consequences of living that out in the dance industry—a place that's both big and small, where news runs free. (Of course, I'm not saying not to date in your industry. I married a dancer, for heaven's sake! Just be careful if you do.)

- Be honest with your partner about your wants and needs, the deal-breakers, and the conversations you need to have.
- If your partner isn't a dancer, introduce them to your career and *everything* it entails. I've seen too many female dancers' jobs be threatened because their boyfriends picked fights with male dancers or choreographers.

37
smoking with children

As I relaxed on the couch, my wife handed me one of her award-winning homemade drinks: bourbon, ginger beer, and a splash of pineapple juice with a tasty Tajín-coated rim.

"Thanks, baby!"

"No problem. Let me know if it's too strong."

A devilish grin spread across my face. "Never."

I held the drink in my left hand while doomscrolling through people's stories with my right. Then the inevitable happened. By clumsily clicking a notification, I accidentally entered someone's live feed. No matter how many times I've repeated this mistake, the feeling remains the same: a loud, anxious code-red alarm in my mind.

Beep! Beep! Get out of there before the host notices you and starts talking directly to you!

In seconds, I was staring at an unfamiliar black man with a low fade. His fly vintage jersey and deep voice made him seem mature, but his mocha baby face gave it away. He couldn't have been older than twenty-one. He was scrolling through the comment section, deciding which to reply to. As my thumbs fumbled around for the exit button, he said something that stopped me dead in my tracks.

"The most insensitive thing is to ask why a victim didn't say anything earlier. I was fifteen. I'm only eighteen now. Even if you all don't believe it, I know what Jeff Thompson did to me."

My vision wobbled like I was aboard a boat sailing through choppy waters. The name the young boy had said echoed through my ears.

Jeff Thompson... *the* Jeff Thompson. It couldn't be.

I scrolled through the comments for any trace of context.

"I'm so sorry this happened to you."

"Jeff is sick."

"You're so strong, Michael. Thank you for sharing your story. We need to air these predators out for the safety of our dance community."

The word "predator" rang like an alarm. I only knew one Jeff Thompson: a phenomenal choreographer from Dallas, Texas. He'd worked with a few artists in his career, but Jeff's claim to fame was his cutting-edge choreography. Because of his unique style, dancers from all over the globe aspired to train with him.

I'd met Jeff a few years ago through my wife, and from that moment on, the three of us were good friends. Whenever Jeff was in town, we'd hang out. Jeff was a sweet guy and had a big heart for those around him. His beauty on the inside matched his beautiful talent on the outside. No way they were talking about the same Jeff I knew.

Or were they? The dance world can feel small yet large at the same time, but what were the odds of there being another well-known Jeff Thompson?

I'd arrived by accident, but this was the first time I watched a live all the way through.

———

"You're a hard man to find!" SHE said as we plopped on the couch.

Though we hadn't asked for anything, Jeff's innate southern hospitality had him handing us cups of water before we could even put our bags down.

"I know, I know. But I'm back now, promise!"

"Where were you this time?" I asked. "Paris? Japan?"

Jeff laughed and shook his head. "Actually, I was back in Texas for a month. Just wanted time with family, you know?"

"Oh, I know exactly what you mean!" my wife and I said, practically in unison.

"Yeah, it felt good to recharge. But I'm not gonna lie. I started to go a little crazy that last week. This country boy needed to be back in the city! So I finally booked my return flight and I've been back for about a week now."

"Ooo, zaddy's back and ready to teach! 'Cause you know the dancers out here are waiting, right?" My wife swirled her cup around like it was an alcoholic drink.

"Ha! You play too much. I am ready. I can't wait for y'all to see one of my new students, Michael. He's amazing. I'm talking the full package. Freestyle, choreography, stage presence. He's going to be a household name for sure."

"Aw, I can't wait!" SHE said.

"Lemme pull up his Instagram so y'all can see. He came to one of my classes a couple of months ago and blew me away. I've been mentoring him ever since."

Jeff handed his phone to SHE, and I leaned into her right shoulder. We watched a video of a tall, lanky boy in the center of a dance class. Seconds passed, then minutes. When the video ended, we swiped through his page to pull up a few more videos.

Jeff's eyes bounced from the phone to us, eager to see our reactions. I succumbed to the pressure and let out a few praises.

"Okay, I see him!"

"Damnnnnn!"

"Oh, he's phenomenal!"

No matter how many compliments I forced out, SHE and I shared the same thought. We wouldn't discuss it until after we left, but through a strange telepathy, I knew she felt the same. We didn't think Michael was that great. He was good, definitely had potential. But the way Jeff talked him up did not match the footage in front of us.

After watching about four videos, the conversation drifted to other topics: Being on stressful jobs. Dance class culture. Freestyle culture. We talked about anything and everything, even about Jeff's adorable hairless cats.

With every new topic, Jeff would bring up Michael again.

"I've been flat-out bullied on jobs. I try to warn Michael about it so he's prepared for the not-so-great parts of the industry."

"Some dance classes turn into video shoots. Publicity stunts. You can't go in just to learn, mess up, and try again. I encourage Michael to stay away from those classes."

No matter the topic, Jeff would find a way to connect it back to Michael. Perhaps he was excited to have a new student. He was known for helping young dancers reach their full potential. But for whatever reason, it started to feel strange. Little did I know that things would only get stranger.

"Y'all wanna smoke?" Jeff held up a tightly rolled joint.

"I'll match you!" SHE tapped his joint with a blunt as if they were saying cheers with glasses of champagne.

"Wait, outside? It's kinda chilly out there. Can I borrow a sweater?" I could feel the goosebumps forming already.

"Of course, come pick one out."

We followed Jeff to his bedroom in the back of the house. When he opened the door, I expected to see a bed, a nightstand, maybe a dresser or two—regular bedroom things. All those items were present. However, something else was in the room. Something I didn't expect to see at all.

As soon as the door swung open, a pair of dark-brown eyes

met mine. They belonged to a young boy with smooth mocha skin, dressed in sweats and a hoodie. He was sitting with a pencil in hand at a school desk with a lamp, textbook, and notebook on top.

"Uh, hi," I said, completely unaware of how else to address this person in the house Jeff hadn't told us about.

Because we'd just sifted through his Instagram less than an hour ago, I knew exactly who he was, but Jeff introduced him anyway.

"Guys, this is Michael. Gotta force him to do his homework. His mom says I'm the only person he'll listen to." He laughed.

I chuckled softly to mask... well, to mask a weird feeling I couldn't put into words yet. All I knew was that seeing this boy studying in Jeff's bedroom at midnight felt strange.

Why is he out so late on a school night? I wondered. At a grown man's house?

"Want this one?" Jeff held up an oversized hunter-green hoodie, interrupting my thoughts.

"Yeah, looks comfy."

"It's snug and soft too!" He handed me the hoodie and turned off the light in the closet. We started following his steps out of the room, but then he paused in the doorway and turned back to Michael.

"We're gonna go have a smoke. Wanna join?"

My mind replayed the question in slow motion. Everything seemed to slow down: my hearing, my vision, and my reaction time.

SHE broke my spiraling thoughts. "Oh, Jeff. I don't smoke with kids. How old are you, baby?"

Her innate southern charm warmed the room. Everyone is baby, sugar, or honey, whether they're older or younger. In this moment I thanked God for SHE's ability to speak up and for her tone, the perfect mix of sweet and stern.

"I'm fifteen, but I've been smoking for a year. My mom knows and lets me."

"Yeah, he smokes with me all the time."

"My love, even if you do smoke and your mom knows, you can do that on your own time, with your own friends that are your age. I don't smoke with kids."

"It's all good, Michael. You can smoke later. You gotta finish your work anyways." Jeff switched his attention back to SHE and me. "In the meantime, we'll take a trip to the backyard and puff, puff, pass."

We smoked and had small talk, and as soon as the blunt was finished, SHE said her goodbyes to Jeff.

"It's getting late and we gotta be up early tomorrow. It was so nice to see you."

"Thank y'all for coming by. I'll be in town for about two weeks, so please come by again."

"Of course, babe!"

We both hugged him, and then Jeff looked on from his porch as we walked to the car. As soon as we closed those car doors, SHE and I exchanged knowing looks.

"What the hell was that?" SHE said, putting her keys in the ignition.

"Some really weird shit. SHE, why didn't he say anything about Michael being in the house?"

"I have no idea. Why did he talk about Michael's dancing like he was the Second Coming?"

"Okay!" I clapped my hands, leaning forward in my seat. "I thought I was being mean or too critical, but no matter how many videos we watched, I thought he was all right. He has potential, don't get me wrong, but Jeff talked him up like he was about to be the next Michael Jackson!"

"That, and him trying to explain why it was okay to smoke with a teenager. No, sir. I didn't like any of it."

As we drove off, a part of me knew this would be the last time we went to Jeff's house.

———

"SHE, come look at this! This is that boy that was at Jeff's house years ago!"

We listened intently as Michael recalled the sexual relationship he'd had with Jeff for years.

"At the time, I thought he cared about me. That's what people do when they care, right? I thought he was my entry into the industry. I was young. I didn't know what grooming was. I didn't know he was taking advantage of me."

My stomach contracted into tight knots.

SHE walked away, shaking her head from side to side. "I knew something was weird that night."

After lots of cussing and walking in circles, SHE only had

one thing left to say. "I'm not blaming myself. From what we saw, it seemed like Jeff was already doing weird shit, so I don't know what I could've realistically stopped. But I wish I would've said more. Or said something, anything, to signal to Jeff or Michael that something wasn't right."

To this day, thinking about that night at Jeff's house brings knots to my stomach.

38
three parts

I answered a Facetime call to see our friend Eliana sobbing into her hand.

"Let it out, friend," I said.

"Oh, Eliana, I know. It's hard to hear," SHE added.

After a few more sobs, Eliana looked into the camera. "They're saying such terrible things about him." She wiped tears from her cheeks, fresh ones taking their place. "Y'all know that's my brother! I just can't believe how everyone's turning on him."

SHE took a deep breath. "Friend, they aren't turning against him. Look, I can't say if everything is true or not. I wasn't there. But years ago, we did go over to Jeff's house late at night and Michael was there. Things were kind of weird. People are standing up for what's right because Jeff had an inappropriate relationship with that boy. And if it's true, I'm sorry, but he needs to go down."

Out of nowhere, Eliana performed an emotional flip. The sobbing ceased, the tears dried up, and she gazed off camera searching for her next words.

"You know, I had a talk with Jeff a couple of years ago. He confessed that he was in love with Michael and said he was a person that didn't see age."

SHE's and my bulging eyes revealed our thoughts, clear as day.

Eliana wiped one more residual tear. "That shit really shook me. I was like, 'Jeff, what are you talking about? That's a *child*. You *have* to see his age, and it needs to stop before you get in trouble.' After that, he told me he would put an end to it, and we never talked about it again."

Silence filled the space where one of us should've replied, but I was too stunned to speak. I couldn't believe what I'd just heard. Eliana knew Jeff was a predator, yet she called us bawling her eyes out because people were saying "terrible things." What about the terrible things he did to that boy?

Before my brain could continue its spiral, my wife put an end to the quiet. "So you knew it was true, sis. Jeff is a thirty-year-old man that knew better. He was my friend too, but he made some bad decisions and now he has to deal with the consequences."

———

Michael wasn't the only person to come forward, and Jeff Thompson wasn't the only predator brought to light that year. From the freestyle scene to the ballet world, dancers from all walks of life were telling their stories of sexual abuse in the community. It seemed like every couple of days a new name was exposed.

Some called it a witch hunt. But because a lot of the predators had several victims, many people celebrated with their hands held high, thankful that these abusers could no longer hide in the shadows. In private settings, I spoke with women who didn't feel comfortable telling their stories, but who were grateful that others had enough courage to expose their abusers. By this time I'd already experienced sexual assault from Elijah, a man who also had other victims. So every morning for about a month, I'd grab my phone and refresh my Instagram feed, wondering if today was the day someone would expose Elijah.

This was an eye-opening time in the industry. Like Eliana, some people buckled down, ready to defend their loved ones till the end. Others immediately denied any attachment to the accused. Then there were the quiet Switzerlands, watching from the sidelines and waiting for everything to blow over.

Another well-known dancer named Anthony held live Instagram sessions each time a new choreographer was in the hot seat. Anywhere from one hundred to five hundred people tuned into these discussions where Anthony took full advantage of the limelight. He'd not only break down the details of the allegations but also teach followers about healthy dancer–choreographer relationships. Until one follower left a comment on one of his live sessions.

"Anthony, you sit here and preach every week about predators and the safety of our community, but you sexually assaulted me."

That was Anthony's last live.

Besides the allegations, the most shocking part of all this was how many people unwaveringly supported the accused.

"What?! There's no way he did that!"

"I've known him for years and he's not like that!"

I'm not saying people are automatically guilty if they're accused. However, if someone wasn't present at the time of the alleged assault, how can they immediately know it didn't happen? People's ability to blindly believe in someone's innocence is jarring. No matter how close I am with someone, if they're accused of any wrongdoing, I'm going to think twice before drawing conclusions.

This past year alone, I found out that two of my most docile male friends had been physically abusing their ex-girlfriends. These were two respectful, mild-tempered young men—at least when they were around me. One of the women had a video to prove her allegations; the other relied on her word against his. Whether that last incident happened or not, these situations serve as stark reminders that you might not *really* know someone.

39

inappropriate relationships

Even after I'd ignored two phone calls, Ms. Erica did not take the hint. She texted me after the second call.

MS. ERICA

Why aren't you answering the phone?
Are you mad at me? Did I do something
in class today?

I didn't *want* to talk. I shouldn't have had to talk, 'cause I was fifteen years old and she shouldn't have been texting a minor in general.

Irritation bubbled up the side of my neck. Nothing was wrong. I'd been quiet in contemporary class because I was tired. TIRED. Going to school and then band practice for two hours, dancing at the studio from 6 p.m. to 9 p.m., studying for exams, and waking up at 5 a.m. to do it all over again... I was WORN OUT.

Ms. Erica never understood how to have appropriate relationships with her students. At the studio, I often watched her call and text students. She gossiped with some of the dancers about other girls at the studio and caused rifts in our team—the same team that set out to "win together" at competitions. She gossiped with parents. Hell, she even gossiped about Mrs. Katherine, the studio owner and the woman she owed all her training to.

From a young age, my intuition buzzed as I watched Ms. Erica conduct herself, but I didn't care too much since she never included me in her drama. Her mess revolved around the older, more talented dancers in the studio and their parents. I was too young and still a novice in my craft; my arches were terrible, my flexibility was nonexistent, and compared to a lot of the other girls, I was at the bottom of the totem pole.

But when I was around fifteen, my technique improved a little and most of the star dancers left the studio, leaving the spotlight on me. I later found out that Ms. Erica was one of the main reasons so many dancers quit. As they peeled away one by one, I somehow became one of the star dancers.

I wasn't as technically sound as some of my peers, but I could perform my ass off. At competitions and conventions, I excelled, drawing the attention of the dance moms, audience members, and ultimately Ms. Erica. She started speaking to me more. She joked with my mom and me more often than ever and asked us for our opinions on costumes and music for competition routines. Quick comments about other parents or dancers escalated into long venting sessions. She gossiped to us about other studio owners, just to spend the entire competition weekend attached to their sides.

Though her actions confused me, I identified her inappropriate traits, noted them, and tried to maintain distance from them. I could speak and listen without being as messy as Ms. Erica. If I could continue to see her through a clear lens, I could focus on my dance training. But when you're around low-vibrational people for sixteen hours a week, it's only a matter of time before they drag you down. It's inevitable.

Just like she'd done with past students, she started texting and calling me. The first time she called me, I was amused.

"Hey, Yorelis!"

"Hey, what's up?"

"Nothing, I just felt like you were off today in class, and I wanted to ask... Are you mad at me?"

My neck retracted in confusion. "No, not at all! I was just distracted. I have a test tomorrow, so all I could think about was getting home to study."

"Oh, thank God! Okay, well, I won't keep you. Good luck on your test tomorrow!"

And just like that, the call was over.

I sat back feeling confused, humored, and everything in between. Ms. Erica really cared that I was mad at her. *Why?* Having been raised in a "Do what I say" and "Stay in a child's place" household, I found the whole ordeal hilarious. I'd never lived in a world where adults cared about how children perceived them. I concluded that Ms. Erica was cut from a different cloth and moved on.

Now, here I was a couple of months later, staring at two missed calls. Ms. Erica was tickling my last nerve.

I inhaled, exhaled, and turned my phone over. I needed to save my energy for important things, such as that essay due the next day, instead of wasting it on an adult without boundaries.

Maybe she'll get the hint, I hoped. *Maybe an epiphany will hit her after the third ignored call. Maybe she'll realize it's not professional to call a minor so late at night.*

All my predictions proved to be terribly wrong, 'cause the next day was a volcano.

I stared ahead blankly at the ballet bun in front of me. Three at a time, we performed across-the-floor exercises. I glanced at the clock in the center of the dance room: forty-five minutes before class was dismissed and I could go home and study for my math test tomorrow. A yawn slipped out of my throat, reminding me of the hours I'd dedicated to my essay last night. I'd planned to study for my math test last night too, but Ms. Erica's calls distracted me, and then the writing took over. Crash-course, last-minute studying was the only option left.

My eyes darted back and forth from the clock. I was eager to go home, take the quickest shower humanly possible, and study.

"Go Yorelis," Ms. Erica yelled, jolting me out of my thoughts. From the moment I'd walked into the studio today, she'd avoided direct eye contact with me. Unanswered texts and calls lingered between us, but my mind focused on the studying in my future.

I looked at the empty dance floor. The ballet bun that had

been ahead of me was now across the floor. My eyes met the face that belonged to the bun.

After a "Five, six, seven, eight" from Ms. Erica, I began the chaînes turns.

"Elbows up! Tight first relevé!"

These were regular corrections for my technique, but on this particular night, they brushed against my already fragile patience.

After the combination ended, I sighed in frustration. Ms. Erica immediately walked over to the stereo and turned it off.

"Yorelis, what did I do? Are you mad at me?"

My jaw tightened as I collected my thoughts. "No, I'm not mad. I'm tired. I stayed up really late doing homework last night and I have to study for a test tonight."

"Are you sure? 'Cause I feel like you're mad at me. Just please tell me what I did."

My ears grew hot. Anger bubbled in the pit of my stomach as my once-fragile patience evaporated. Somewhere in the furthest part of my brain, I knew these feelings were mostly due to exhaustion and demanding schoolwork, but this was the straw that broke the camel's back.

"Erica, I'm not mad at you. And even if I was, it SHOULDN'T matter. Why? Because I'm fifteen. A kid. A minor. Someone you shouldn't be calling late at night, or at all for that matter."

The more I spoke, the more the volcano bubbled. My volume rose with each word until the inevitable eruption. "You're unprofessional and inappropriate. Coaches shouldn't care if their students are mad at them. If you think I have an attitude, talk to my mom—not me! I. SHOULDN'T. BE. DEALING. WITH. THIS. SHIT!"

"Oye," my mother interjected, bass overpowering her tone. As soon as she noticed her child clapping her hands with every syllable, she managed to slip into the back of the dance studio. She remained observant, allowing me to say my piece to Ms. Erica. However, she drew the line at my cursing at an adult.

"No faltas al respeto," she said. *Don't disrespect.*

Mami took over after my blowup and talked with Ms. Erica, who gave me a heartfelt "I'll change" apology. Business continued as usual, except that she now walked on eggshells around me during class.

But from that night on, I knew what I had to do. Nothing could change my mind. I knew it was my last year at that dance studio.

———

Ms. Ericas are everywhere. Plenty of other dance studios, conventions, teachers, and coaches blur the line between adult and child. In this case, my teacher wanted to be my friend— texting my phone at all hours, allowing my opinion to dictate her choreography choices, gossiping about fellow dancemates. Though it was stressful, I thank God she had only tried to be my *friend.*

One afternoon during my sophomore year of high school,

my friend Taylor pulled me into an empty girls' dressing room just as I was about to go to my next class.

She whispered, "Come here! I gotta show you something!"

Taylor was a dance major like me. We wore leotards and tights for most of the school day and spent the rest in academic classes, but we attended dance studios that were on opposite sides of Tampa.

"What?!" I matched her intense whisper.

"Okay. I got something to tell you..."

"Girl, come on! What?" My patience was crumbling.

"Okay, okay. So me and Ronald are talking..."

"Ronald?! Forreal?! *Talking* talking?"

In our teenage-girl world, there was talking to someone, and then there was *talking*. This was one step past friendship, closer to an intimate relationship. If you were *talking* to someone, you'd be hanging out a lot, spending a long time on the phone or messaging apps, and making a deeper connection.

Ronald was a freestyler, hip-hop dancer, and teacher in the Tampa Bay area. Because hip-hop teachers were hard to come by, a lot of studios shared teachers. My dance team coach, Dreama, traveled all over Tampa during the week. One day she'd be teaching in North Tampa, the next she'd be moving and grooving with kids at a studio in South Tampa. On Wednesdays, she'd teach classes at my home studio in Town 'n' Country.

Besides a couple of random master classes, Ronald didn't teach at my home studio, but via the internet, I could see that he led a teaching life like Dreama's. He taught at Taylor's studio and others, had a photography and DJing business on the side, and threw battles for the freestyle community.

"Shh! You can't tell anyone!" Taylor whispered. "But yeah, we've been talking for a couple of weeks now. He asked for my number after class."

"Oh, shit. That's crazy, Taylor! Have y'all done anything?"

"No, not yet, but I know he has a chode."

My head launched back as my cackle shook the dressing room walls. (Just so we're on the same page, a "chode" describes a man's penis when it's short and wide in girth.)

Regaining my composure, I asked Taylor, "Wait, how do you know?"

"'Cause he sent me a picture."

Before I knew it, I was looking at a pixelated picture of Ronald's penis on Taylor's flip phone. The reveal sent me into a new, more ravenous fit of laughter.

"I CANNOT believe he sent you a picture! Girl, you are crazy!"

I knew Ronald. I'd booked a photo shoot with him my freshman year and attended some of his battles. He was a cool guy and a really talented dancer, but he was also a *grown-ass man*.

Teenage logic and a lack of education clouded my judgment. I saw nothing wrong with Taylor and Ronald's relationship. In fact, the secretiveness around it excited me. But as time passed, Ronald's name continued to circulate around the community. I'd hear rumors about him talking to underage girls, and I knew these rumors were facts because the girls were my friends. By my senior year, even more names had been added to the list, forcing me to come to the obvious conclusion: He was a predator. He crossed lines no dance teacher should cross with their underage students.

———

Mimi's home was like a time machine. From the moment I walked in, it flooded me with memories of my childhood home. Mimi lived in California while I grew up in Florida. The exterior of her home didn't resemble mine, but the inside was all too familiar. Mimi was the middle child of three girls, aged eleven to eighteen, so hair products, sparkly clothes, and vibrant personalities filled the home, overpowering the presence of the girl's brother. When they weren't speaking to me, the girls often bickered with each other—the unspoken rite of passage of sisterhood. Their home always made me feel nostalgic and brought a smile to my face. It was necessary medicine for me, a young adult living thousands of miles from her family.

Mimi displayed an abundant amount of personality with her mom and sisters, but she was dead silent around me and even more reserved in her dancing. That never bothered me. It was why I was there in the first place, to give Mimi private lessons and help build her confidence and technique. You gotta start somewhere! Lord knows I did.

Mimi's demeanor didn't concern me at all—until her mother pulled me aside after one of our lessons.

"I'm sorry about Mimi. She's always been timid, but it's gotten so much worse since she left Priscilla's dance company."

"What do you mean? What got worse?"

"Her confidence. That's why she's so scared to dance. Priscilla got into her head. Said some really crazy things to her."

"Scared to dance? What did Priscilla say?"

And in no time, I was reading the Instagram messages Priscilla had sent to Mimi:

"You aren't going to improve outside of the company."

"The previous training you may have received was okay, but I got you to this level. You're making a huge mistake leaving the company."

"You could've been a star. Your technique and training will suffer."

My heart ached. This woman had tethered a child's gifts to her dance company. She tried to convince Mimi she'd fail without her instruction—and nearly won. It took some months and multiple dancers and teachers to pull Mimi out of that funk, but she finally had a breakthrough.

That entire setback, however, could have been avoided if an adult—Priscilla—had messaged another adult—Mimi's mom. From there, her mother could've dealt with the situation and decided how to move forward, whether she would've shown Mimi the messages and turned the situation into a life lesson, or shielded Mimi from reading the messages and instead focused on the future dance teachers in her life. But whatever could've happened remains theoretical, all because an adult decided to overstep their boundaries with a child.

———

Inappropriate adult–minor relationships can occur in all kinds of ways. Many form right under our noses. They hide in plain sight, camouflaged in places that are supposed to be safe for children, such as a school, a dance studio, or a sports team. Hell, I read a story about a therapist who was exposed for sexual misconduct with some of his teen patients. The thought of predators in spaces that are supposed to be safe havens is gut-wrenching.

We have to do better. Speak to one another. Keep our eyes open for signs.

I don't have children of my own yet, but I have watched my friends communicate with predators. Though they weren't my teachers, I exchanged inappropriate messages with a couple of people who were well into their twenties when I was a teen. So, because of my perspective, I can provide some general rules to help keep our children safe. These rules might be obvious to some, but not to all, so bear with me:

1. Surveil their devices.

You should know who's texting or calling your child. Tons of apps, software, and phone-carrier parental control options allow you to see who your child is communicating with.

2. Monitor social media.

Get the login information for every social media account your child has. If you choose to, you can negotiate a certain age where this rule expires, maybe sixteen or seventeen.

3.   Stay hip! Try to remain "in the know" when it comes to new apps and social media platforms.

As a former sneaky kid, I can confidently say that kids can be *very* sneaky. Some apps present themselves as one thing but contain a world of different uses. I was blown away when I learned about one popular app that looks like an unassuming calculator—until you enter a code and the app takes you to a vault. There, you'll find a place to "safely" store nude pictures.

Talk to other moms or young adults to stay updated. As a twenty-seven-year-old with no kids who struggles to stay hip, this is easier said than done. But I promise, we got this!

4.   Monitor your children's interactions with adults.

All communication regarding your child should go through you. Any emails, texts, or calls from an adult should go to you. This is one of the most important pieces of advice in my opinion. I've seen firsthand how a simple "Practice is at 9 p.m." text from your child's coach can escalate down the road.

For a more conservative approach, you may ensure that no adult outside of your immediate family has your child's phone number. For a more liberal approach, maybe an adult can message your child if it's in a group chat thread—a "Dance rehearsal is canceled" text arriving to both you and your child at the same time.

To me, a child is anyone under eighteen. But I also understand the importance of gaining trust with our children and preparing them for the real world, so by all means, shift these rules as they creep up to eighteen.

5.   TALK TO YOUR KIDS.

Like the previous rule, this rule is of top-tier importance. *Talk to your kids.* Teach them what abnormal behavior and misconduct from an adult looks like.

If your child participates in extracurricular activities, be specific to those activities. For example, dance is a sport that requires contact. If my leg is turned in or my foot is sickled, it's normal for a teacher to physically correct my form. Discuss how an appropriate touch differs from an inappropriate touch. Maybe choose a dance studio that has observer windows for the parents to watch the class. Sit in on a few classes to build your trust in that teacher. Even if your child doesn't do an extracurricular activity, talks like these can improve their interactions with adults in school and in family settings as well.

This rule is important for children because it's a seed—their first lesson in boundaries. Our definition of boundaries will shift and change as we get older, but understanding our boundaries is necessary for our well-being. It will allow us to navigate children–adult relationships and, later on, adult relationships with coworkers, bosses, intimate partners, and friends. By then, we should have a good idea of boundaries. Like roots firmly planted in the ground, we'll know our limits and vow to keep our roots in the earth. Then things will happen to challenge the strength of those roots.

"Slipping into someone's DMs" is practically a rite of passage in the age of social media. You see an attractive person on Instagram and send a message demonstrating your interest in them. Sometimes it's a cute and harmless "What's up?" or "How are you?" Other times, it's a little bolder, like "You got a man?" Then there's the virtual catcalling line, "Hey, sexy."

When done the right way, slipping into someone's DMs opens a door that allows you to get to know someone comfortably. It can serve as a cute space for light flirtation if you're interested. It can go south, depending on the person, but it can also be an exhilarating time. That is, until your boss slips into your DMs.

Some choreographers in this industry are notorious for slipping into dancers' DMs. If one thing's for sure, it's that dancers talk—*a lot*—so those names float around our large-yet-small industry like particles in the air.

———

Another text notification illuminated my phone.

GIANNA

He's messaging AGAIN.

A sigh left my lungs as I started typing.

ME

What's he saying?

GIANNA

He's asking if I want to have some wine in his hotel room. What do I say?

My eyes nearly rolled off my face.

ME

Gianna, it's okay. We already talked about this. Tell him you're tired and you want to rest for rehearsal tomorrow.

When she started this job, Gianna wanted to know as much as possible about her new work environment. Because I had done a job with this artist before, she had no problem coming to me with all her questions.

"How's the artist?"

"Are the female dancers mean?"

"Are the men respectful?"

I didn't want to talk badly about people, but I also wanted her to be as prepared as possible.

"The women are chill. We're goal-oriented, so egos aren't really an issue for us in rehearsal. The wardrobe department head was an ex-dancer, so sometimes she talks about the dancers to other dancers, but don't pay her any mind. I think she just likes to stir the pot. The men are really respectful; I kick it with them a lot. I've heard rumors about the choreographer flirting with the female dancers, but he hasn't tried me. Keep that in the back of your head so you aren't caught off guard if it does happen."

Gianna was now witnessing the rumor become fact. My phone buzzed again.

GIANNA

Okay. He said to have a good night and that he'll see me tomorrow. But what if he tries me again? Would he fire me for not flirting back?

ME

Don't stress about it. There's no way he
can fire you for that. If he tries you
again, tell him you have a boyfriend.
He'll back off. Even if you don't have a
boyfriend, make one up. Act normal in
rehearsal. Say hello, but don't give him
too much so he doesn't get the wrong
idea.

GIANNA

All right, thank you so much. I feel so
much better.

I slammed my phone onto the bed. Tears pushed against my
eyes from the feeling overwhelming my body. The feeling of
sheer guilt because I'd typed nothing but lies.

Everything I said was a lie. A big, fat lie. I'd heard stories
about women being fired for not putting out. Some men don't
give a shit about your boyfriend. And even if you're the epitome
of professional, some men mistake politeness for flirting. Gianna
could follow every rule I gave her and still be harassed. That
reality frustrated me to no end. I was glad she felt better. I was
glad that these rules could ease her anxiety. But I loathe the fact
that this is a common conversation among women in the work-
place, whether they're in the dance industry or not.

Here are a few tips I wish I could've given Gianna:

1.   Be clear.

When you express your lack of interest, be as clear as possible. Don't leave any wiggle room for other interpretations. You
also shouldn't have to make up a fake boyfriend.

2.   Don't be afraid.

It's easier said than done, but try not to be hesitant. Don't be afraid to establish those boundaries.

3.   Say "Fuck this job."

If you continue to feel uncomfortable, leave. If you're fired, then fuck that job. It clearly wasn't the right work environment for you.

40

thank you for not trying to fuck me

It's customary for dancers to speak to the teacher after class. So as soon as the class finished, everyone rushed up to Bryson to show their gratitude, introduce themselves, and ask for notes.

I had every intention of speaking with Bryson, but first I had to run to the restroom to change out of my sweaty clothes. Damp clothes not only make my skin crawl, but when combined with cold AC and a nighttime breeze, they make it that much easier to get sick.

After changing into dry clothes, I entered the dance studio to find that most of the students had already spoken to Bryson. Only three dancers were left in line. I grabbed my bag and joined the line, but as soon as Bryson saw me walking nearby, he stopped talking to the person in front of him and addressed me.

"Aye, you're so cold!"

He walked toward me with his arms open, and I returned his hug.

"Thank you so much, for real! I'm glad I was finally free to take a class from you. Your choreography is timeless."

"Thank you, thank you. But *you*." He fanned out his arms as if he were praising a queen. "Why haven't I met you? You're a beast!"

"Thank you!" I said again, humbled by his praise. "I don't take class a lot, but when I saw that you were teaching, I couldn't pass up the opportunity to learn from you."

"What's your Instagram? Imma hit you up. I have to work with you."

To say I was excited would be an understatement. I was absolutely *floored*. Bryson is a legendary choreographer in the industry. No matter how good I get or how many accolades I'm blessed with, I'll always hold a tender spot in my heart for those who came before. Those who made the things I'm doing possible. Some of the work he created inspired me to pursue this career in the first place. Fast-forward years later, and there I was, standing in front of him as he sang my praises. It was the kind of full-circle dream only God could make come true.

He handed me his phone, and I typed my name into the search bar.

"Here you go!"

As he grabbed the phone, my wedding ring caught his attention. His eyes widened and his neck retracted. Then he reached down and, with his index finger and thumb, lightly pinched my wedding ring. *Pinched* my wedding ring! And if that wasn't weird enough, he looked back up at me, clasped his hands together, and said nothing.

"All right, well, Imma head home now." An awkward yet polite smile spread across my face. "Thank you again for the class. Nice to meet you."

"Nice to meet you too, love."

As I drove off, I called my wife and recounted the events. We laughed together, and then I filled her in on the rest of my class experience—award-winning choreography and the delightful surprise of industry friends dancing alongside me.

After multiple therapy sessions and talks with my wife, I can make light of the situation. But the truth is, years ago I would've been livid. Having cursing fits alone in my car, frustration turning my cheeks pink and pushing tears out of my eyes. All because that interaction with Bryson ignited an insecurity I'd dealt with for a long time: Do you *really* like my dancing? Or do you just like my face? It's a tale as old as time in the life of Yoe Apolinario.

When I was fifteen, I won my first freestyle battle. The prize was two hundred dollars and a photo shoot with the event coordinator. At the beginning of the shoot, he praised my dance and congratulated me on the win. Throughout the shoot, however, he instructed me to look at him as if he were my lover and groaned after I did so.

Back in my "grinding to move to LA" days, I called off work and missed out on vital money because a hip-hop teacher from Los Angeles was teaching a masterclass. I drove an hour to Orlando in an unreliable car, using gas I didn't have the money for, to get a taste of my dream. A peek into what life could be.

After the class, the choreographer sang my praises till he was blue in the face, only to slide into my DMs later to let me know how sexy I looked the night before.

When I first got into the freestyle dance scene, I jumped at every opportunity to sharpen this newfound skill. Late-night sessions thirty minutes away on a school night? The obstacles didn't matter because I wanted to reach my full potential.

For the most part, the community welcomed me with open arms, complimenting my fusion contemporary hip-hop style. Because the scene was still male dominated at the time, I never thought twice about men asking to session with me. That is, until I ended up at a "session," which is a group event, with just me and a man, no music, and countless invasive questions about my love life.

If I included every little story about a male dancer or choreographer expressing their love for my dance and then pursuing me shortly after, we'd be here all day. I quickly realized that my gifts were only going to get greater, and by the grace of God, I'd only be getting prettier. To stop questioning the validity of my gifts, I needed to find coping mechanisms.

Now when men compliment my art, I study their body language. I look for prolonged eye contact, wandering eyes scanning my frame, and whether they linger after everything's said and done. Asking for my number instead of my social media is a tiny red flag. Late-night direct messages raise an eyebrow. Commenting with heart-eye emojis and liking all the posts that don't include my wife are monumental red flags.

I also play a waiting game. Will our future interactions be respectful, or will he take a chance one day? A few men have shown their support for my craft, shown respect, and then one day, boom. They're messaging me late at night about how beautiful I am. So before I get too comfortable, the waiting game tells me everything I need to know.

When I lived in Tampa, I met a well-known dancer from South Florida named Kidd. We knew each other vaguely via Facebook, but we'd never met in person. Then on a humid night outside of an Ybor City club, he introduced himself and professed his steadfast love and support for my dancing.

"It's so nice to finally meet you. You're one of my favorite dancers, hands down."

He repeated this multiple times, and then did so again later in the caption of a picture he posted of us.

For weeks following, he commented on my videos with stars and praising-hand emojis. He reposted my videos with the same caption: "one of my favorite dancers." Kidd overwhelmed me. First off, by that time in my life, I'd never received admiration from a man in the way he showcased it. I was still early in my freestyle journey, so while I was good, I wasn't exactly top-tier yet. The community in Tampa is honest. They'll sing your praises for your hard work and growth, but they won't go above and beyond. Kidd was going above, beyond, and to the stars.

With my imposter syndrome and lack of training, I couldn't believe someone enjoyed my art *that* much, so my brain went elsewhere: *Does he really like my dancing? Or is he just saying all these things to get close to me and later pursue me intimately?*

I decided to play the waiting game. With every posted video, dance event, and session, I waited and waited to spot the tell-tale signs, but they never came. Kidd never shot his shot. He was an actual fan, just like I was of him.

———

A few days after the class with Bryson, I scrolled to a video from my friend Mari. She'd taught a collab class with Bryson the month before and had just posted the footage from the class. The caption read, "Got the opportunity to work with a legend in the game. I've looked up to you for years, so when you asked to teach a collab class, I couldn't believe it was true. Thank you, Bryson! I had an amazing time working with you!"

I'd worked with Mari on quite a few jobs, and we'd grown close through the years. I knew she would be honest with me, so I called her.

"Hey, Yoe! What's up?"

"Nothing much, boo! I'm good. I just called 'cause I wanted to ask you a question."

"Go ahead, sis."

"So... Bryson. How...? Was...?"

"Ha! Listen, the women in this industry don't play about me! You're the fifth person to ask me about Bryson. Working with him was good. Do I think he'll take a chance if I show an ounce of interest? Hell yeah. Did he? No."

"Damn right we don't play about you! He's got quite the reputation and I saw a peek of it after I took his class one time, so I just wanted to know how your experience was."

"Well, I'm not gonna lie. While we were texting to set up rehearsal times, he was a little flirtatious. He'd end messages with 'beautiful' or send heart-eye emojis. But during our first rehearsal, I deadened all of that."

"How?"

"Girl, as soon as we got into that studio, I said, 'Thank you so much for asking me to teach with you and believing in my choreography. A lot of the male choreographers that ask to work with me are really just trying to fuck me. So thank you for not being one of those."

My brain practically broke, malfunctioned, replaying the monumental words Mari had uttered: *A lot of male choreographers that ask to work with me are just trying to fuck me. So thank you for not being one of those.*

"Mari!" I yelled into the receiver. "Ugh, that's the smartest thing I've ever heard! What in the reverse psychology?!"

Mari cackled into the phone. "Exactly! After I said it, that man started sweating, trying to respond. 'Oh, no, really? That's what they do? I would never do that.' Blah blah blah."

The two of us giggled like schoolgirls for the rest of the phone call. Our conversation bounced between lots of subjects, but in the back of my brain, Mari's response to Bryson continued to play on a loop.

Half of me fangirled over the sly way she'd encouraged Bryson to act better without lecturing him or cussing him out.

With only a couple of sentences stated at the beginning of the rehearsal, Mari had ensured her safety. That wisdom has been in my arsenal ever since.

The other half of me brewed with distaste, a sour feeling in both my mouth and stomach. Mari's words were conniving and smart, but deep down, I hate that female dancers have to check on each other via private texts and phone calls. I hate how often female dancers are pursued for all the wrong reasons. And most importantly, I hate that when I was on the phone with Mari, I was taking notes, conjuring up ways to ensure *my* safety.

———

No matter how many times I talk about these things, being open about my experiences with men in this industry gives me anxiety. I can practically hear the array of reactions as I type.

"Wow, men really do that?"

"Not all men are like that."

"Women abuse their power sometimes too." (While I completely agree with this thought and have also seen it first-hand, people can use this kind of statement to downplay men's actions.)

"People are so sensitive these days. It's like you can't even talk to a woman anymore."

One of my most consistent prayers is that God continues to surround me with men outside of that toxic mold. I know they exist. I've seen the proof time and time again. Despite my sexual orientation, I believe that men and women need each other. It's balance. It's the way of life. I pray that I can continue to find good-ass men to be my friends, family, and role models for my future children.

However, I'm faced with the reality that no matter how uncomfortable it gets, or how much anxiety it gives me, I have to talk about these unfortunate run-ins with men. It lets other women know they aren't alone. It opens the conversation about what's appropriate and inappropriate. It ignites thought and self-work in the men who want to do better and lead others down the same path.

41

the first woman

The fluorescent lights, blank walls, and wooden floors made me feel like I'd never left. I set my bags down and unpacked all the necessities: my foam roller, amino acid supplements, foot massager, and muscle rub. It had been three months since our last show with My Way, Usher's Vegas residency, and time had flown by. Now here I was, two weeks into rehearsals for a new show. Instead of Caesars Palace, this time Usher would be gracing the stage at Park MGM.

We finished teaching and staging acts one and two. We'd made a few changes, but overall the show was very similar to last year's. Because act three was comprised of ballads and smaller dance numbers, Rio, the choreographer, skipped to act four—the high-energy finishing act of the show. Hits like "Yeah!," "OMG," "DJ," and "Scream" filled the set list, easily making it one of the hardest sections of the show.

The previous year, I had a very unique role in the show. I was a tomboy, Usher's lesbian best friend who always tried to steal his women. Half male, half female dancer. In acts one and two, I danced with the men in their sections. While all the women wore heels and tight dresses, I sported a two-piece suit, a crop top, and Air Force Ones. During the twerking sections, I posted up with the male dancers as our characters gawked at the beautiful women on stage. When it was time to partner up for a sensual salsa number, I was assigned the male role then too. In the acting moments between big sections of choreography, my character flirted with all the beautiful women around me. And by the time act four rolled around, my character had transformed entirely. I finished the show as a female dancer, wearing a tight bodysuit, performing the twerking sections, and partnering with male dancers.

Because acts one and two hadn't changed too much, I expected act four to be no different. Rio told us to spread out so we could start going over the choreography for "Yeah!"

"Are we wearing wigs again?" I asked, referencing the elaborate wigs the female dancers had worn the year before.

Rio shook his head. "No, there won't be any wigs this year. But that doesn't matter for you anyway. This time you're gonna be a boy the whole show."

My muscles twitched as I struggled to hide my excitement. The only response I managed to blurt out was, "What? Um... Okay!"

I learned the rest of the male sections—the demanding jumps, slides, and athletic choreography. The same choreography that had inspired me when I was younger. I thought I was dreaming, and it didn't end there.

After going through act four, it was time to learn the legendary piece "You Make Me Wanna...", a sexy male dance number specifically tailored to the women in the crowd. There are chairs, suggestive movements, ab muscles on display, and lots of other grown-man activities. Think Chippendales but with black men and R&B. Like *Magic Mike*, but it's Usher so you can't even compare them! It's one of the moments in the show where, instead of larger-than-life staging and lights, a single spotlight highlights each male dancer. Instead of being in a formation behind Usher, the men are positioned in a straight line beside him in a simple yet effective display of strength and power.

This number only requires four male dancers; we had six. They were going to make cuts, and I'd just gotten there. So, while the rest of the men took the floor, I sat down to watch. The camp was already breaking barriers by making me a male dancer, so there was no way they'd cast me in—

"Yoe, you'll be in the third chair."

"Huh?" I choked.

Rio chuckled and placed the third chair in line, right off of Usher's shoulder. "You're doing 'You Make Me Wanna...'. You're gonna be the first woman to ever do it."

————

It never gets old. Every night as I sit in that chair, posed and waiting for my spotlight to illuminate the stage, I feel it. I feel audience members in the front row darting their eyes between Usher and me, the million-dollar question written all over their faces: Is that a woman? As they begin to realize, some of them smile, point, and talk about me.

While performing the steps, I feel my star quality thrive. A testament to God's gifts and all the hard work I've devoted to my craft over the years. I feel the fruits of that labor. I think about my first hip-hop class. I cringe remembering how bad I was when I started freestyling. I'm grateful for all the odd jobs I worked just to get out of Florida.

Most importantly, I feel the energy of all the female dancers like me—the queer ones, the tomboys, the ones who don't like suggestive choreography, and the ones who prove that they can not only hang with the men but smoke them while doing it. Those women, though I may not know them personally, push me every night. When I'm tired, sore, or not feeling my best, they push me. They remind me of the barriers I've broken and am continuing to break. They remind me of the history I'm making.

42

the beauty

I have quite a few horror stories under my belt, some of which I chose not to include in this book. I've had bad times in the past, but those experiences don't represent my career. They'll never trump the highlights, the beautiful moments God has granted me through this avenue of art and dance.

I'll never get over the feeling of performing in a sold-out stadium, my body pulsating from the roar of screaming fans. When I was younger, I dreamed about traveling around the world and meeting other dancers and artists. Traveling for any dance-related event with all expenses paid—airfare, hotel, food per diem—seemed like a fantasy. When my social media followers send me pictures of campaigns or commercials I've been in, I still get butterflies in my stomach.

I didn't know how many doors dance would open for me. The young woman working relentlessly to save up to move to

LA just wanted to dance behind artists and in music videos. She had no clue she'd end up building Yoe, her own brand—a personality and talent people will tune into with or without a musical artist. She didn't know you could actually make a living off of dance. Shoot, she figured she could pay rent and a couple of bills here and there, but purchasing property in the over-priced Los Angeles housing market? Somebody go back in time and let her know.

When I was younger, I looked up to the contemporary dancer Ashley Gonzales. The YouTube video of her 2010 solo "It's Gonna Be a Long Walk" has ninety-one thousand views at the time of this writing, ten thousand of which I'm sure I'm responsible for. From her movement quality to her commitment, she blew me away the moment I discovered that video. I knew she was based somewhere in California, but nothing would prepare me to meet her a couple of years after moving.

"You don't understand! Your movement was so different, unlike anything I'd seen before. Especially in Tampa," I told her.

Having transitioned fully into foundational hip-hop, I hadn't trained in contemporary in years, but I didn't care. Adult Yoe left the building, and fifteen-year-old Yorelis stepped in.

"It blew my mind and continues to, because you're still phenomenal. I just can't believe I met you."

I can't believe I taught workshops in Israel or got lost in Japan because I couldn't read any of the signs. To this day, I can't believe I know Alyson Stoner, that once-little girl dancing in a Missy Elliott video who showed me kids can do this too, inspiring me to take my dance training more seriously.

Contrary to the antics you read about in some of these chapters, the dance industry isn't all terrible. I've been blessed to work with wonderful dancers, choreographers, and artists. Dance has allowed me to add stamps to my passport I never thought possible. I've experienced beautiful full-circle moments that reminded me I'm right where I'm supposed to be.

Grateful is an understatement.

acknowledgments

I'd like to thank my beautiful wife, Sheopatra. Thank you for listening to all my crazy thoughts and dreams. When I make you drop everything to read a new chapter, or ramble on about an idea for a novel out of nowhere, you never shy away. I am eternally grateful that out of all the people in LA, God chose you.

Thanks to my family for raising a tough, independent thinker who's in touch with her emotions but doesn't take shit from anyone. Because of y'all, I've survived and thrived.

Thank you to THECouncil, the tribe of women that make me feel safe in this city. My family away from my family. No matter what it is—exchanging, praying, dreaming, or crying—you guys are there for me. The sisterhood I never knew I needed, but now I can't imagine life without.

To my followers and supporters, THANK YOU! Finishing my first work, *Café Con Leche*, was the first triumph. Holding the book in my hands felt like a dream come true. But all of your positive reactions and uplifting reviews pushed me to continue with this passion. The opportunity to get my stories out there and touch others, all while adding income to this freelance lifestyle, is something I do not take lightly. Whether it's my dancing, merch, books, or lifestyle content, you all continue to pour into me. Please message me or email me. I'd love to continue to get to know y'all more.

There are some stories I didn't include in this book. Things I'm not yet ready to talk about yet. Experiences I don't know how to put into words. At the same time, my story is not over. I still have years left in this city. At first, adjusting to and navigating the dance world were my priorities. Now, I'm moving into choreography and producing while nurturing my marriage and planning to start a family. More stories are in the works, experiences I hope to write about and let you all in on. Stay tuned.

about the author

Yoe Apolinario is a Tampa, Florida native, but currently resides in Los Angeles, California. Most of her days are spent working as a professional movement artist, dancing behind artists in music videos, concerts, and commercials. During free time she's usually loving on her wife and pets, or reacquainting herself with one of her first loves, writing.

instagram.com/yoe.apolinario

tiktok.com/@yoewrites

keep up with yoe!

https://linktr.ee/yoeapolinario

want more?

If you like romance novels, stay tuned! Yoe is working on something new and exciting to bring her readers!

also by yoe apolinario

Available on EverythingYoe.com